Navigating Trauma in the English Classroom

Navigating Trauma in the English Classroom

Adam Wolfsdorf
New York University

Kristen Park Wedlock
Georgian Court University

Cassandra Lo
St. Thomas Aquinas College

NCTE

National Council of Teachers of English
340 N. Neil St., Suite #104, Champaign, Illinois 61820
www.ncte.org

Staff Editors: Kurt Austin and Cynthia Gomez

Manuscript Editor: Michael Ryan

Interior Design: Jenny Jensen Greenleaf

Cover Design: Beth DeWilde

Cover Images: Jeff Hobrath/www.vecteezy.com, Erica Simone/Getty Images, and chaiyapruek2520/Getty Images.

ISBN 978-0-8141-3268-5 (paperback); 978-0-8141-3269-2 (ebook)

Library of Congress Control Number: 2022947730

Dedication

This book is dedicated to our students,
without whom none of this work would be possible.
The ones who learned with us and the ones who taught us.
The ones who showed up and the ones who shared their stories.
We are forever grateful.

Table of Contents

Acknowledgments

Cassandra would like to acknowledge and thank her husband Zachary Craig, her mom Andrea Lo, her late grandmother Edith Rosso, her best friend Christina Cleaver, her mentors Dr. Elizabeth Dutro, Dr. Meenakshi Gajria, and Dr. Ebony Elizabeth Thomas, her WOC sisterhood in academia, especially Dr. Victoria Gill and Dr. Grace Player, and the two smallest additions to her life—her baby Xavier and a little bearded rescue dog named Lola.

Adam would like to acknowledge and thank his wife and life partner, Inga Blom, for her steady, grounded support; his dynamic sons, Dax and Jett, for their unstoppable exuberance and extraordinary spirits; his parents, Gail and Joe, for their steadfast commitment to education and diligence; and his mentors Mike Dealy, Emery Gross, Donald Wiedis, Sheridan Blau, and Ruth Vinz, for their vision, passion, and belief. To these people, he is eternally grateful.

Kristen would like to acknowledge and thank her writing and life partner Matthew Wedlock, her daughter Shae River, her parents Theresa and James, her brother Robert, her therapist Shay Stanton Shwahla, her co-collaborators and conspirators Jenna Kotch, Marie Roguski-Safain, Katie Ingegneri, Jessica Hagemann, Marci Mazzarotto, Jade Lascelles, and Heather Goodrich, and her mentors Ruth Churchill, Denise Blackstone, Jeff Friedman, Bobbie Ellis, Deborah Metzger, Laura Jelly, Michelle Naka Pierce, Melissa Buzzeo, Veglahn, J'Lynn Chapman, Bhanu Kapil, Reed Bye, Connie Chismar, and Jessica Hausmann.

Cassandra, Adam, and Kristen would like to extend a thank you to Robb Clouse, for bringing us together on the screen and through the page. We would also like to thank Michael Ryan for his remarkable copyediting and superlative humanism. And, of course, thank you to Kurt Austin, Cynthia Gomez, and NCTE for getting behind this project and believing in the work.

Preface: "A Matter of Infinite Hope"

"It's hard to believe in coincidence, but it's even harder to believe in anything else."

—John Green, *Will Grayson, Will Grayson*

The funny thing about this book is that it wasn't even our idea. We weren't planning on writing a book; we were planning on a presentation. Even that isn't entirely accurate. We were ambivalent. It was COVID—the universe had paired us together in a joint NCTE session . . . on Zoom! We didn't know each other. Actually, Cassie and Kristen knew each other. They had worked together for two years at Georgian Court University. But I (Adam) didn't know them, and they didn't know me. We had applied for NCTE's 2020 *¡Confluencia!* Conference, and NCTE had determined our thinking was analogous—that our visions on trauma and pedagogy were aligned and should cohabitate. But even that wasn't enough. Honestly, we'd been on the fence . . . presenting on Zoom . . . "maybe wait until 2021" . . . but then the second coincidence came—the one that finally flung us together, concretizing an inevitable partnership that, prior to that moment, hadn't really been a partnership at all.

On November 6 of 2020—a Friday—while I was quarantining in agrarian northern Connecticut, and Cassie and Kristen sheltered in place sixty miles from each other in their respective homes in New Jersey, an email came in that instantaneously obliterated whatever distance had separated us. At 10:19 p.m., while I sat on my sofa streaming season six of the *Great British Bake Off* . . . while Kristen nodded off putting her daughter, Shae, to bed . . . while Cassie remained riveted to CNN and the election results that would decide the fate of the world for the next four years . . . Robb Clouse of NCTE clicked send on his mousepad, delivering the following message that would unite Kristen, Cassie, and me forever:

> I'm interested in learning a bit more about your co-presentation at our upcoming *Confluencia* convention—Trauma in the College English/Composition Class—and the possibility of a professional book on the topic . . . depending of course on the focus, your interest, etc. I'm curious how it may be similar to or different from other approaches, the research base and, if you are indeed interested in publishing on the topic, how that might be further developed (single author, coauthored narrative, edited, etc.). I'd love to learn more—the topic of trauma continues to receive increasing attention in K–12 schools and concomitantly teacher education courses, and we may well still be ahead of the curve a bit with the latter. (November 6, 2020)

Life is a funny thing. Its best and worst moments often come at us out of nowhere. We hope for the promotion. We fear the cancer diagnosis. We pray for the big raise. We tremble at the unexpected car crash, the hospitalization, the foreclosure. But life doesn't unfold like that. It doesn't obey our hopes and fears. It doesn't hold a mirror up to our deepest desires and our most lurid trepidations—it gives us new ones we haven't anticipated. Hedwig delivers Harry's invitation to attend school at Hogwarts. Lucy feels snow at the back of the wardrobe. Khalil gets shot. Amir watches Hassan in the alleyway. Dorothy reunites with Auntie Em. Almost everything miraculous and devastating in life falls outside of our expectations. We fear this, we get that. We strive for this, but then that happens. It's why we live, and it's why we read, too—because we don't know what happens on the next page.

In 2015, I was a Teaching Fellow in Kenyon College's summer writing workshop for teachers. On the second-to-last day of the program, I attended a talk lead by David Lynch, editor-in-chief of the *Kenyon Review*. David spoke about writing: "good writing will surprise you even when you know what is about to happen" (August 12, 2015). The same is true for life. Even when we know the plot, the plot will upend us, sweep us off of our feet, and land us upside down in a pile of "how did that happen?!"

When Robb Clouse sent that email, it initiated a convoluted, carnivalesque marathon sequence of events that would begin with Zoom call ideas, introductions, and awkward beginnings and would materialize into 150-plus pages of words, words, words. We were interested in trauma. We knew that. We were living through a pandemic. We knew that, too. We suspected but didn't know for sure—or have any real way of predicting—that our ideas, formulations, and conceptualizations about trauma would align and interconnect in ways that felt spontaneous, dynamic, and, ultimately, cohesive.

Lastly—and perhaps most important—we knew English teachers were struggling. We'd spoken with them about their experiences navigating trauma in the English classroom. We had our own uncertainties, ambivalences, confusions, and despairs. Trauma was real. Trauma was everywhere, and it wasn't going away. If anything, as the months of the pandemic labored on, it was getting worse. What would the English classroom look like on the other side of Zoom living? How would we prepare for it? What did we owe to our students and to ourselves? And what about the thousands of other English teachers and professors across the country? What would they do, and how would they do it?

Perhaps English teachers had read about it? Perhaps they had gone to workshops or participated in faculty development training sessions? But from conversations we'd had with colleagues—and from our personal research—it seemed clear that there was a problem: students had trauma histories, texts dealt with trauma, but English teachers had not been given sufficient training when it came to thinking about, responding to, and engendering classroom environments and cultures where trauma could be assimilated and dignified without being parceled into overly prescribed "solutions" that felt either too conveniently simple or too frustratingly convoluted and vague.

So, that's what we are trying to do in these pages: to talk about trauma as it relates to the English classroom. This book will not be perfect. It will not turn you into a world-renowned trauma therapist. It will not, necessarily, even make you better capable of handling trauma in the English classroom. It might make all of this even more difficult, confusing, perplexing, and disorienting. But we do believe that your choice to read this book says something important about you—that you are reading this because you care about your students and seek to learn more about how you can support, understand, and help them. Furthermore, we hope your journey into these pages will allow you to feel more at ease and masterful when it comes to the highly complex and layered experience of teaching English within a community of individuals, many of whom may have been traumatized, some of whom suffer from PTSD.

If we can do that . . . if we can be the 150-plus pages that help you feel more prepared to handle students in crisis who get triggered, retraumatized, or volunteer personal narratives of trauma in your classrooms, then we believe we will have succeeded in our collective attempt at writing about a topic that, like the dragon in so many mythical legends, cannot quite be slain. Among Cassie, Kristen, and I, we believe that understanding trauma and learning to work with it represents the journey of a thousand miles. We hope this book proves to be one of the important steps you take en route. And even if there is no exact destination, together we can help each other traverse a treacherous landscape that, even if it does not lead us all the way back to Kansas, invariably may bring us a little bit closer to home.

I

Consumption

1

What Is Trauma, and Why Should We Care?

What is trauma? Why should we care? How can we think about it, and in what ways does it play out in our classrooms? In the following chapter, I (Adam Wolfsdorf), attempt to look at and answer these highly complicated, layered, and nuanced questions. As English teachers, we are—perhaps more than any other type of educator—uniquely positioned to share content and receive student narratives that center around trauma. And yet what structures, educative tools, and practices currently exist that prioritize trauma awareness and education for English teachers? This chapter will begin the exploration of trauma in its many levels, layers, and dimensions. It will serve as a springboard for the rest of the book, beginning a journey that has no real beginning and may, in fact, never end. That said, here goes! Welcome to Navigating Trauma in the English Classroom.

> If anyone on the verge of action should judge himself according to the outcome, he would never begin. Even though the result may gladden the whole world, that cannot help the hero; for he knows the result only when the whole thing is over, and that is not how he became a hero, but by virtue of the fact that he began.
>
> — Søren Kierkegaard, *Fear and Trembling*

In 1999, the first year I ever taught English in a classroom, I was teaching American literature to a group of high school juniors. We were reading Jack London's short story "To Build a Fire," one of the first narratives written about Alaska. For those who have not read it, "To Build a Fire" tells the story of a newcomer to the region, an unnamed man who sets out to complete a full day's hike on the Yukon Trail in the middle of a frigid winter. The temperature on the day of the journey is minus 75 degrees, 107 degrees below the freezing point. Foolish and thoughtless, the man sojourns on despite multiple warnings. He is accompanied only by his dog, the Alaskan husky. As the man mindlessly trudges forward, the dog senses that the journey is perilous. It is a cautionary tale about man's ignorance and hubris in the face of nature's superior power.

For as long as I live, I will never forget what Windsor did that day.[i] As we were engaging in close reading and discussing the text, suddenly raised her hand. She was a timid girl who did not often speak in class. Although she was not poor, she tended to dress in a disheveled manner. She had matted brown hair that was usually frizzy and unwashed. When her hand rose, I could sense the eagerness—she had something very important to say.

"Yes?"

"I just find it . . . " she began and then had to gather herself to speak because she was almost shaking. "I just find it so horrible what this man is doing to that dog."

She took a breath. "He just . . . he just keeps abusing it and abusing it. It's like he won't stop."

Her classmates turned to her. Taken by her intent interest and focus, I also found myself suddenly captured by her interpretation.

To be clear, there is no specific language in London's story that suggests the man is actively abusing the animal. One could argue the very fact that he forces the dog into such inhospitable conditions is an act of abuse—and it may very well be—but seemed to be suggesting a different type of abuse: a hostility and active mistreatment that might be analogous to the type of thing a child suffers when she is being beaten by a parent at home.

Suddenly something clicked in my brain. This wasn't about the literature. It wasn't about the man and his dog. It wasn't about Alaska, Jack London, or the Yukon Trail. It was about. She seemed to be trying to tell me something, to tell the whole class. She seemed to be confessing that something horrible was happening at home. What that something was, I have no idea. I never found out, and I never will. But she had opened a door and allowed me to peek into whatever disturbance was operating in the secret chambers of her home life. I had become, for the briefest of moments, a witness to 's trauma.

As we continued to read and discuss the text, and, indeed, for the rest of the year, I could not help but wonder what type of sadistic treatment might be enduring at home. Whenever she showed up for my class, the thought percolated at the back of my mind. When I passed her in the halls, it was there, too. But it was vague. Even now, as I sit here writing this book twenty-three years later, the thought still tingles in my brain. If somehow were the victim of a perpetration that the text was somehow triggering in her, then what was I, as her English teacher, supposed to do? In the most innocuous sense, she was merely giving a literary interpretation—a reading of sorts. Should I have asked her to more specifically divulge what she had begun to share? Should I have headed over to consult the school's guidance counselor based on a comment she had made about Jack London's man and his dog? Should I have let it go? Turned a blind eye? I had twenty other students in that class to worry about. And four other classes as well, each with twenty or more students in them. Was it appropriate to move in? What if I did, and she ended up telling me her father was sadistically beating her? Or raping her? Or . . .

All this occurred almost a quarter-century ago. Trauma, as Ray Kinsella states in *Field of Dreams*, wasn't even a "glint in (my) eye" (Robinson, 1989). I hadn't written fifteen articles on trauma in the English classroom. I wasn't the Humanities Chair at an independent school I helped to build and develop. I hadn't spent three years directing a master's program in teaching of English at Columbia University. I hadn't been on faculty at NYU, where I train English teachers at both the undergraduate and graduate levels. I hadn't served as a Visiting Assistant Professor in the graduate liberal studies program at Wesleyan University. I hadn't endured two and a half years researching and writing my dissertation, which looked at trigger warnings in relation to literature. (Trigger warnings weren't even a "thing" that educators talked about.) And I hadn't written this book. The person who taught "To Build a Fire" to Windsor was a first-year English teacher just trying to figure out the classroom. Grading my first papers. Creating my first seating charts. Figuring out my own life. Trauma . . . I had no idea what trauma did to people, how it could get triggered in the English classroom, or what to do about it if it did. I had gone into the field on a whim—I loved reading; I loved writing; I adored working with students. I wasn't married. I didn't have two children. I was making thirty thousand dollars.

But even then, in the infancy of my own professional development, I knew what had communicated about the man and the dog was significant. I knew that once I understood what she was telling me, I would spend the rest of that academic year knowing something painful about her life. If I put 's confession on a balance against my hopes and dreams for what these students might learn and discover in my American literature class, it seemed fairly clear to me, even then, that 's story was far more important and troubling than anything I had diagrammed in my curriculum. All of this I realized. But what I did not know was what to do with what I had learned.

In the course of a lifespan, most people will confront trauma. Even for those fortunate enough to come from secure homes with loving, supportive parents, trauma is a fairly predictable eventuality. From Ancient Greece and the Roman Empire to the Civil War, Emancipation, and even today, with a seemingly ceaseless global pandemic and a Russian invasion of the Ukraine, this has always been the case. From the big T traumas such as car accidents, domestic abuse, global pandemics, sexual assault, racial discrimination, and teaching and learning behind masks, to the small t traumas of recurrent emotional abuse, bullying, break-ups, and microaggressions, trauma is a force that places a considerable burden on our lives (Howell and Itzkowitz, 2016). Sometimes there is more. Sometimes there is less, but always it is there—not a maybe but a definitely, a fact of life, even a rite of passage for the individual who walks through the world and comes to understand and experience it in all its vicissitudes.

In *The Body Keeps the Score: Brain, Mind, and Body in the Healing of Trauma*, Bessel van der Kolk argues that trauma changes the brain (2015). Heinz Kohut believed that trauma shatters the individual, fragmenting the self, such that the resources at hand are insufficient to meet the demands of the moment (1984). Martin Heidegger believed in the existential analytic, the idea that trauma is built into the natural architecture of life. Just as we will experience joy for the birth of a new child, feel inspired by an extraordinary painting, or laugh uncontrollably at an exquisitely clever joke, so too will we grieve and shudder at a sudden and unanticipated horror: the loss of a loved one, the doctor's diagnosis of cancer, the witnessing of a racial injustice. As Khalil Gibran notes in *The Prophet*, our joys and our sorrows are often interwoven and interconnected: "Your joy is your sorrow unmasked. And the selfsame well from which your laughter rises was often filled with your tears" (33). In *Hamlet*, the Player King speaks: "Where joy most revels, grief doth most lament; / Grief joys, joy grieves, on slender accident" (3.2.198–99). Robert Stolorow, the psychoanalyst and philosopher who lost his wife to cancer, referred to trauma as "the unbearable embeddedness of being" (22). Buddhist psychiatrist Mark Epstein, a clinical assistant professor at NYU, stated, "If we're not suffering from post-traumatic stress disorder, we're suffering from pre-traumatic stress disorder" (2013).

And yet, despite its prevalence, trauma is still tinged with a sense of the taboo. The student survivors in our classrooms will often feel shame, doubt, and inferiority. They will sequester their traumas in private spaces, locked away, believing they will be shunned, ostracized, or held responsible for the perpetrations of others. For a Windsor, who may have endured significant abuse at home, why does this shame exist, and why do survivors feel obliged to suffer in silence rather than opening up and setting their burdens free?

This denial of trauma—a psychological silencing of the lambs—is a reality of mainstream education. Although our classrooms are peopled with individuals who come to us with a history of sexual, physical, emotional, and racial abuse, so little is done to prepare educators for the classrooms that they teach and the survivors they are bound to serve. Research conducted by the Centers for Disease Control and Prevention indicate that:

> (O)ne in five Americans was sexually molested as a child; one in four was beaten by a parent to the point of a mark being left on their body; and one in three couples engages in physical violence. A quarter of us grew up with alcoholic relatives, and one out of eight witnessed their mother being beaten or hit. (van der Kolk , 2015, 1)

If we extrapolate these statistics to the seventy-five million students who people our kindergarten through doctoral level programs in the United States, we can conclude that roughly fifteen million students have been sexually molested; almost nineteen million have been beaten by a parent; another roughly nineteen million have grown up among alcoholic relatives; and close to ten million have witnessed their mother being beaten or hit.[ii]

Let's pare that down further to make it even more personally relevant. I teach in New York. The average New York City classroom accommodates thirty-five students. If the CDC's data are accurate, then here are my stats:

- 7 have been sexually molested
- 9 have been beaten
- 12 have parents who engage in physical violence
- 9 have grown up among alcoholic relatives
- 4 have witnessed their mother being beaten

In fact, in urban populations where there might be higher stress levels and increased incidents of domestic violence and abuse, the numbers may be higher.

A majority of teacher education and teacher training programs focus disproportionately on content and curriculum. Even the prestigious doctoral program that I graduated from in 2017 concentrated almost exclusively on pedagogy in terms of its relationship to content—aesthetic techniques for teaching poetry, short stories, and novels. I loved the program; I loved my professors; and I am a far better educator as a result of that experience. But there was not a single required course aimed at helping doctoral students understand the psychology of students who come to us carrying the wounds and bandages of abuse and trauma. Somehow, the mental health realities of students are recognized (if they are recognized at all) as the purview of school psychologists and on-site social workers.

In my twenty-three-year career working with and training English teachers, I've found that too many are absolutely baffled by how to handle, think about, or respond to student trauma when it becomes obvious that an individual in their classroom has been triggered (Wolfsdorf, 2017). During my doctoral research, I interviewed an English department chair with fifteen-plus years of teaching experience. An impressively fluid thinker, he became completely tongue-tied when I asked him what his position was on trigger warnings when teaching literature. Following a thirty-eight-second silence, the veteran teacher stumbled through almost four minutes of completely incomprehensible ideas, filled with numerous "ums," a handful of contradictions, and several more strange, unsettling pauses. In all of its verbal disfluency, the response said so much: he did not feel equipped to handle trauma in his English classroom. Nor did he know how to train his own English faculty on how to respond to student trauma when it surfaced. He was not alone.

To be clear, trauma is something that all educators face in the classroom. And yet the question of trauma may be especially significant for English teachers—particularly for English teachers and professors working at the secondary and post-secondary levels, where students are beginning to develop the cognitive capacities for recognizing and paying testimony to their personal narratives.[iii] Unlike less aesthetically charged content spaces (Rosenblatt, 1938; Greene, 1988) such as chemistry, math, and statistics (and none of this is said to take anything away from these centrally important and meaningful fields), English dives deliberately into an experiential dyadic with the very soul of trauma. Hester Prynne stands upon the scaffold. Alison Bechdel discovers that her father is gay. Sethe gets raped. Lolita is kidnapped and repeatedly molested. Hamlet contemplates suicide. Elison's protagonist, an unnamed black man, is the victim of repeated racial trauma. When the English teacher cracks open the spine of the novel, a continuous sequence of traumatic narrative will unfold: Ishmael, Nick, Celie, Gregor Samsa . . . these are the literary protagonists who pay testimony (Felman and Laub, 1991). The stories they tell are rife with conflict and filled with hardship. As I wrote in a 2019 article for *English Journal*:

> It's hard to imagine a single literary text worth teaching to high school students that doesn't delve deeply into some controversial topic. Take *Hamlet*, for instance: What happens if the Danish prince does not contemplate his own mortality, if Claudius does not kill Hamlet Sr., and if Ophelia does not end up drowning herself in a pool of tears? Gatsby: unrequited love, obsession, murder, substance abuse. *Huck Finn*: slavery, racism, abusive parenting, and religious indoctrination. In the high school classroom, controversy equals opportunity. One of the roles of the high school English teacher is to be courageous enough to bring elephants into the classroom—heavily laden topics so incendiary that they shake students from the comforts of their normative experiences, push them to reconsider their own ideologies, and—through significant, intelligent risk—bring about real changes in thought and experience. (29)

The type of literary texts we teach in the English classroom nosedive directly into traumatic spaces. The words are often beautiful, the language exquisite, but peel away the linguistic beauty, and what lurks beneath is often the leviathan (Hobbes, 1962). Though not a therapist—and it is *very important* to clarify that the English teacher should not attempt to play the role of mental health professional—the English teacher will often teach texts that narrate the type of traumatic circumstances that shatter people's lives, stress characters beyond what they can tolerate, and fundamentally alter their ability to feel safe and cohesive in the world (Kohut and Golberg, 1984).

And our students will respond to what they read. Most will be able to tolerate the intensity. Many, even if they have experienced analogous traumas to the characters on the page, will cope just fine, may benefit therapeutically from the work—such as Yana. Mere months after her father's sudden death, I taught Yana *Hamlet*. Because Yana came to class consistently, was a dedicated and hard-working student, and reliably contributed to class discussions and maintained an A average, I had no idea she was coping with a tremendous loss. I only found out about the loss after we'd completed the play. Yana showed up to office hours, asking me if I would read her college essay. When I read the essay, I almost fell out of my chair: it was a narrative about her father's recent death. I'd spent the past ten weeks rhapsodizing over the beauty and profundity of *Hamlet*, completely oblivious to Yana's pain. The following day, I approached Yana with shame, eager to check in and see whether reading the play had unwittingly retraumatized her (Wolfsdorf, 2021). To my great relief, Yana relayed that reading *Hamlet* in the wake of her father's death had felt therapeutic, a valuable way for her to process the loss. But perhaps Yana was unusually resilient? What about other students who read and write about texts that tap into their personal traumas? Will such encounters with reading and writing feel therapeutic for them, too, or retraumatizing?

I'm reminded of Alison, who needed to walk out of my classroom at Teachers College because I showed a video featuring a car crash. I would discover that Alison had suffered a near fatal car crash the previous year. These stories are not unusual. As Elizabeth Dutro explains in her article "'That's Why I Was Crying on This Book': Trauma as Testimony in Response to Literature" (2008): "I was 16, sitting in junior English, when my teacher, with her usual style and drama, began reading the first lines of Karl Shapiro's poem about sudden trauma, the tragedy of innocent lives cut short" (423). It was Dutro's first week back in the classroom following her younger brother's death, and the poem was simply too much for her to process at the time. As we move through this book, we will hear more stories about student survivors who are asked to sit through exposures to literary content that directly mirrors some of their own traumatic experiences. Is this good? Bad? Therapeutic? Harmful? Regardless of what it is, it is *inevitable*, and we need to know how to handle it.

And it is precisely the inevitability of trauma's place in the English classroom that makes this book so essential. We cannot—and must not—attempt to sanitize or whitewash our classrooms. We must not ban books or censor content. As English teachers, our job is difficult; the narratives we teach often contain extreme and triggering content. Oedipus, Ophelia, Paul Baumer, Esther Greenwood—are characters who face intense circumstances. And yet, it is perhaps because of their hardships and not in spite of them that these characters and their worlds demand our attention. As Maya Angelou writes in *I Know Why the Caged Bird Sings*, the hardest and most devastating stories are the ones that need to be told: "there is no greater agony than bearing an untold story inside you" (2008).

As English teachers, our job is paradoxical. Though in life, it is wise to actively avoid trauma, in the English classroom, we deliberately seek it out, finding the books, the poems, and the plays that give trauma the opportunity to speak. Look at Khaled Hosseini's opening to 2003's *The Kite Runner*:

> I became what I am today at the age of twelve, on a frigid overcast day in the winter of 1975. I remember the precise moment, crouching behind a crumbling mud wall, peeking into the alley near the frozen creek. That was a long time ago, but it's wrong what they say about the past, I've learned, about how you can bury it. Because the past claws its way out. Looking back now, I realize I have been peeking into that deserted alley for the last twenty-six years. (1)

It is the novel, invariably, that gives the caged bird the right, at last, to sing. Ishmael. Sonny. Nick Carraway. Pecola Breedlove. They give testimony and we, the reader, serve as witness (Felman and Laub, 1991). As the story is told, the will to know and to utter aloud overcomes the will to deny, abstain, shield, or hide. As Theodore Reik states: "(t)he repressed memory is like a noisy intruder being thrown out of the concert hall. You can throw him out, but he will bang on the door and continue to disturb the concert. The analyst opens the door and says, 'if you promise to behave yourself, you can come back in'" (Reik as quoted in Mack, 2014, 43). When the caged bird sings, it breaks the silence that nullifies it. As Judith Herman writes in *Trauma and Recovery*: "(t)he conflict between the will to deny horrible events and the will to proclaim them aloud is the central dialectic of psychological trauma" (1).

Every day in classrooms throughout the United States, English teachers share these stories with their students: "Shooting an Elephant," *Orpheus and Eurydice, Beloved*. The trauma is ripped open and entered into, thirty-five students and a teacher in a 900 square-foot classroom. Desks in a row. Lithonia lighting overhead. Two windows slightly ajar. The sound of wind cutting through the leaves and honking taxi cabs. Johnny's staring at Suzy. Wendy's got a headache. Jamil's biting his lower lip. Tyrelle daydreams. Sal's asleep. Marty and Rick text underneath their desks. Phillipe, Sean, and Jennifer are tuned in while Dr. Davis reminds them that things fall apart, and the center cannot hold. Ophelia's losing her mind. Ahab hunts the white whale. They're reading about a trauma, but they don't even know it. They're in the belly of the whale, and nobody realizes that their name is Jonah.

And students have their stories as well. At times, they will write essays analyzing the green light or examining industrialization and economics in *Death of a Salesman*. But other times they will speak to us from the shadows of their own personal lives. They will tell us about their father's problems with alcohol, about the time they were sexually assaulted, or about their own forays into drugs or illicit sexual behavior. Either unwittingly or intentionally, they will convey their secrets. And in these moments, the traditional structure of teacher/student dynamics will break down—like it did with Windsor—because what is being shared goes beyond footnotes, grammar, spelling, and punctuation. And once these boundaries are broken, in some ways they will always be broken. If Jamilla tells us she has been raped, or Juan writes about the time his father threw him onto the floor and whipped him with a belt, we as English teachers cannot simply choose to unlearn what we've learned. For both the student who shares and the teacher who listens, the relaying of the traumatic event represents an act that is often indelible.

What This Is and What It's Not

The central argument of this book is that English teachers who understand trauma-informed pedagogy (Dutro, 2008; Felman and Laub, 1992) are far better off, both for their curricular content and for their students, than are English teachers who do not take the time to learn about how trauma operates and can get triggered through reading and writing. And yet, while we argue for English teachers to become trauma informed, we also emphasize that we are not advocating English teachers attempt to play the role of the therapist. Though it may be tempting at times, and though our students may seem to need us—or we may feel attracted to the idea of helping them in this way—we are by no means qualified to take on this role. My wife is a clinical psychologist. She spent seven years in graduate school, did four years of externship, one year of internship, and an additional year of trauma-specific fellowship training. She is a director of training for psychologists at Lenox Hill Hospital in New York City. And even now, in her fifteenth year of practice, she gets supervision and is supported by a team when she is handling the complicated trauma of some of her patients.

Cassie, Kristen, and I are not attempting to compel you to hand in your favorite novels and open up a private counseling practice. We know our limitations; we hope you recognize yours as well. As my former mentor and dear friend, Sheridan Blau, once explained to me, "the English classroom should be therapeutic but not therapy." Navigating the fine line between responsible, empathetic teaching and indulgent, unproductive enmeshment is one that takes English teachers years to master, if they master it at all. We must, of course, be warm, sensitive, and student centered, but we must also know how to create firm boundaries and some level of empathetic distance so that our students know we care but do not get seduced by the idea that we are here to treat and heal them.

We do not need to heal students or be their therapists in order to use what we know about trauma to foster English classrooms where students are better attended to, embraced, and served. The extensive research that Cassie, Kristen, and I have done on English teachers navigating trauma in their classrooms has made it increasingly clear that a book of this nature is filling a significant need. In recent years, the issue of trigger warnings and their relative value (more on this in chapters 2 and 3) has highlighted a desperate need in educational circles to provide some measure of security and perceived safety for student survivors. Unlike any previous time in history, the matter of student mental health has become a priority (Wolfsdorf, 2018; Wolfsdorf, Scott, and Herzog, 2019; Wolfsdorf, 2021), and this was true even prior to the COVID-19 pandemic that has gripped the world for more than two years. Student mental health remains a significant feature of classrooms throughout America.

As we have become more "trauma conscious" (van der Kolk, 2015, 349), and as the taboos attendant to student trauma and mental health have dissolved, an urgency in academic spaces has asserted itself: English teachers (and, really, all teachers) should learn some level of trauma-informed pedagogy. As with the recent acceleration of DEI training that has become ubiquitous, trauma-informed pedagogical practices may be more relevant in the twenty-first-century classroom than ever before. With the disruption to and reconsideration of the white hegemonic patriarchy that has overarched classroom cultures and set arbitrary norms for pedantic curricular aims, concern for the psychological well-being of students has simultaneously advanced itself and become a central feature of progressive pedagogy. With adolescent suicide on the rise, psychopharmacological drugs used by one in every four teenagers, and what will certainly be years or even decades of PTSD for large numbers of students emerging from this pandemic, we as English teachers owe it to our students to become more mindful and aware when establishing classroom cultures that promote growth and empathy for survivors.

In the pages that follow, we will not be so bold as to imagine that we possess the solutions to these incredibly intricate and, at times, intractable issues. But we do hope we might provide a framework and possible ways for English teachers to more comprehensively think about and more confidently account for the type of student responses that can be triggered by exposure to literature or shared (intentionally or unintentionally) through student composition. We hope to help you create a classroom space that encourages deeper inquiry and clearer, braver (Arao and Clemens, 2013) textual encounters, both for the students we teach and for us as educators. Many of the English teachers we have worked with, supervised, and researched have been rattled and confounded by instances of student trauma. Like the students who themselves feel shattered and overwhelmed, many of the English teachers we've spoken with have expressed how they feel out of their depth and ineffective. Can this book help you to be more effective? Can it bolster your awareness so that when survivors get triggered in your classroom, you feel you have a steadier, more comprehensive approach? We think the answer is yes.

As we move through this book, we want to make it clear: we are not advocating for neat, packaged, and fully delineated solutions. Given what Cassie, Kristen, and I have learned about trauma, to do so would be a dishonest act, an arbitrary manipulation of an entity that often defies our overt attempts at mastering or completely understanding its messy boundaries and borders. Trauma is a highly complex space. As Susan Banitt writes:

> Traumatic events, by definition, overwhelm our ability to cope. When the mind becomes flooded with emotion, a circuit breaker is thrown that allows us to survive the experience fairly intact, that is, without becoming psychotic or frying out one of the brain centers. The cost of this blown circuit is emotion frozen within the body. In other words, we often unconsciously stop feeling our trauma partway into it, like a movie that is still going after the sound has been turned off. We cannot heal until we move fully through that trauma, including all the feelings of the event. (23)

Like many of the trauma-informed pedagogical experts who have come before us (Dutro, Felman and Laub, Britzman, Caruth), we hope our contribution can make the path easier for you. Not fix the road, but give you a better set of boots with which to walk on it.

We believe that if English teachers better understand trauma—how it behaves and misbehaves, how it might get triggered, and what it does to our students and ourselves—then we will most likely be more prepared when students in our English classrooms get triggered by difficult content or seem otherwise shaken, hyper-aroused, or shattered. Like a good boot camp, which does not prevent war but rather prepares you for it, we hope the pages that follow will serve as a training ground to take you deeper into the complex layers of trauma, shining a light into that dark space, Virgiling your Dante in the descent to more fully understand trauma's underworld.

The Road Ahead

Structurally, this book is divided into three main sections. Part One of this book, *Consumption,* will focus primarily on reading literature. It will provide a comprehensive overview of trauma: what it is, how it operates, and why understanding it can help English teachers become more empathetic and responsive when student trauma gets triggered by encounters with literary content that runs analogous to student experiences. To do so, I will provide a brief history of trauma, both within and beyond the classroom, and attempt to provide the reader with a heightened sense of utility when it comes to the educator's ability to recognize, conceptualize, and respond to student trauma, should it surface. In Part One, I will also focus on trigger warnings and demonstrate how content warnings, though well intended, may not provide the comprehensive "protection" they claim. Finally, I will demonstrate through sharing case studies involving former students how engaging with literature can trigger as well as prove therapeutic for traumatized survivors.

Part Two, *Declaration*, considers the impact trauma has on classroom relationships, assignments, and writings. It will highlight the importance of relationship building between teachers and students, especially when engaging students in activities and assignments that could be triggering. Part Two will also focus on how composition and writing activities can serve as areas for witness and testimony within the English classroom, and how instruction around "high stakes" assignments such as the college essay can support students when they write about difficult topics. Additionally, Part Two will address how to respond to and assess trauma narratives by proposing feedback strategies and rubrics that acknowledge the risks students take when sharing deeply personal stories.

While Part One and Part Two lay the groundwork for defining what trauma is and how it shows up in the texts we read, the papers we grade, and the classrooms we lead, Part Three, *Embodiment*, emphasizes the inner work required of instructors who choose to engage in trauma-informed pedagogy. Just as consuming literature helps the reader understand the relationship of a character to their trauma narrative, meditation invites a person (the educator in this case) to understand their relationship to their personal story—attracted, averted, attached, detached, nonattached, embodied, disembodied. Part Three shares the neuroscience of meditation and the cognitive science of memory to unpack the way that trauma registers in the body-mind-heart and how people can learn to read their personal trauma narratives. While trauma disrupts the projected arc of the story, meditation interrupts the attachments to stories. Techniques from contemplative arts are offered for replenishing the individual instructor, whereas techniques from narrative medicine are shared for building resilient communities of instructors. Finally, Part Three closes with a section addressing the concept of teacher burnout, ultimately proposing instructor self-care and community support as potential antidotes.

Although we acknowledge and recognize that trauma awareness, mindfulness, and recovery should be thought of as a lifelong process, one replete with a myriad of components and foundational elements, we hope this book will be experienced by its readers as one of the formative texts that facilitated and shaped the sojourner's authentic quest for better understanding, rethinking, and ultimately deeper comfort with both the burdens and opportunities endemic to working with traumatic experiences in the classroom.

2

Alison, AT&T, and the Neuroscience of Trauma

Many of our students have been traumatized. Recent statistics from the Centers for Disease Control and Prevention indicate that perhaps 90 percent of students have experienced one or more traumas. But when and how did these traumas occur? The reality is, we usually don't know—nor, necessarily, should we. But what happens when we do know? What happens when, through a moment of sharing or discovery, we find out that a student has endured a particular trauma? And what happens when something that we do or prioritize in the classroom taps indirectly or directly into a student's personal trauma history? In this chapter, I (Adam Wolfsdorf) examine one such moment that occurred when I was teaching in an English education graduate program in the summer of 2015. Utilizing this particular circumstance, I navigate the highly complex interface between student trauma and personal pedagogy. In the process, I explore the neuroscience of trauma, hoping to shed better light on what happens to students' brains, bodies, hearts, and emotions when they get psychologically triggered by content in an English classroom.

> "'You're a rotten driver,' I protested.
> 'Either you ought to be more careful or you oughtn't to drive at all.'
> 'I am careful.'
> 'No, you're not.'
> 'Well, other people are,' she said lightly."
>
> —F. Scott Fitzgerald, *The Great Gatsby*

In my memory, it happened on Tuesday, July 21st. The 21st of July was a hot, humid day in New York City. How hot? I can't remember precisely. But I know it was hot. Hot enough to make the subway ride up to Teachers College (where I was in the process of completing my doctorate) relatively unbearable. Hot enough to make you want to duck inside, avoid the outdoors, pray for fall. According to Google—which never lies—New York City rose to a sweltering 89 degrees on that midsummer Tuesday afternoon. I could have been at the beach. I could have been sipping margaritas by the pool. I could have been watching Masahiro Tanaka throw fastballs to David Ortiz. But I wasn't. I was standing in front of a group of English ed graduate students at Columbia University, teaching them about the intersectional space between literature and drama.

Fifteen years earlier, I had gone into teaching, excited about having summers off, sunbathing along the French Riviera, hiking into the Grand Canyon, laying out a towel along the beaches of Martha's Vineyard or Block Island. But somewhere between twenty-five and forty, these desires had become less significant to me, had been tucked away into the recesses of my past the way that scratch and sniff, Atari, and ColecoVision had been tucked away. On July 21st of 2015, fifteen years into my career, I was choosing, by some mysterious force within, to duke out the heat in a lecture hall up on 120th Street and Broadway. It was the summer of 2015, and my life as an educator was about to change forever.

That summer I was the coordinator of InSTEP, a Columbia University master's program for inservice English teachers. For three weeks every July, approximately fifty graduate students from around the world journeyed to Columbia University for a three-week immersion into the most progressive techniques in the field of English education. Affiliated with Lincoln Center and the Metropolitan Museum of Art, InSTEP rooted its approach in aesthetic education and the work of Maxine Greene. Earlier that same year, I had actually been a student in the last class Maxine Greene ever taught; on our second-to-last class, we showed up—Maxine did not. She had died quite suddenly the night before, succumbing to pneumonia. InSTEP aimed to further her legacy. In the summer of 2015, we had students from Houston, Taiwan, Florida, Egypt, Bangladesh, California, the works. Between 9:30 a.m. and 3:30 p.m. Monday through Friday over three intensive weeks, we immersed ourselves in the thinking and pedagogical practices of John Dewey, Maxine Greene, Louise Rosenblatt, Lisa Delpit, Ernest Morrell, James Moffett, and others.

On July 21st, we were in the final week of the program, and I was instructing a teaching of drama course to a group of fifteen students in their third and final summer of the program. For their summative assessment, I had tasked my students with adapting a short story into a two–three-minute short film. In teams, the students would direct, act, and edit their projects and then share them on the final day of the course. As fortune would have it, Dan Blaney, a childhood friend of mine and an executive producer at a major advertising agency in Manhattan, had shared with me the final cut of an AT&T commercial that he and his colleagues had recently wrapped. The piece was remarkable: an "It Can Wait," don't-text-and-drive campaign AT&T had shot along the suburban streets of Los Angeles.

The commercial focuses on a young boy who witnesses a dramatic car crash. The crash occurs when a mother, who is driving her six-year-old daughter to a birthday party, takes her eyes off the road and looks at her phone. Her car swerves over the midline, smashing head-on into a pickup truck. Bouncing off each other, the vehicles spiral up into the air, flip and then crash back onto the road. Glass shatters, metals dent in dramatic, topsy-turvy cacophony. As this occurs, a boy on a bicycle looks on in wide-eyed horror at the dramatic, unsettling catastrophe. AT&T's message is unmistakably clear: *it can wait.*

July 21st was day two of the one-week, thirty-five-hour intensive course. An hour earlier, we had broken for lunch, but now it was nearing 1 p.m., and the students were returning. I set up the projector and queued the video clip. With students' short films due Friday, I believed the AT&T commercial would be a helpful model and spur ideas among them. And it probably was helpful—except for the fact that it wasn't.

I don't know exactly what I said to introduce the clip. It was eight years ago, and memory is tricky. As Barbara Kingsolver states, "Memory is a complicated thing. A relative to truth, but not its twin" (Kingsolver, 2013). That said, I believe I led with something like:

> I'm going to show you an ad that one of my close friends produced. It's a great example of narrative compression. Hopefully the ad will give you all some good ideas for your film projects. It's quite an intense piece.

Like I said, that's what I remember saying. I was in the middle of a seven-hour teaching workshop. The pressure was on. Fifteen Ivy League students sat in a semi-circle, glaring at me, needing me to be *exceptional*! I was supposed to be smart. I was supposed to be engaging. I was supposed to be the one capable of capturing and maintaining their focus between the hours of 9:30 a.m. and 3:30 p.m. in the middle of a torrid summer. Was I up for the task? Could I do it?

Although I do not recall the exact words I used, I do know that I purposefully left out the fact that the footage included a car crash. The car crash was the reveal—the arresting, cataclysmic event. Like Biff walking in on Willy Loman's affair, or Oedipus realizing that he has killed his own father, I wanted the commercial to surprise and unsettle them. The crash was arresting, unnerving, and destabilizing; it was supposed to shock the viewer, to shake the witness from the womb of their personal comfort zone. In his Poetics, Aristotle argues that the purpose of art is to dislodge us from the comforts of mental equilibrium—to arouse and unsettle (Aristotle and Halliwell, 1939). Arousal leads to catharsis, and through catharsis the soul is cleansed and purified. By saying very little, I was honoring Aristotle. After all, the students had spent more than fifteen-thousand dollars for the summer; I wanted them to get their money's worth. Saying as little as I could, I pressed play, and the film began to roll . . . and that's when it happened.

Alison Scott was a student in the classroom that day. She had wavy red hair, a freckled face, and a keen, penetrative nature. Alison had a perfect GPA and was considered by many within Columbia's faculty to be one of our best students. I found out later that Alison had scored a perfect 1600 on the SAT. Throughout the program, she'd asked pointed questions, taken steady, comprehensive notes, and been an exceptional contributor to class discussions. By all accounts, she was an extraordinary student.

The tables in the lecture hall were arranged in a horseshoe shape; I stood at a lectern at the opening of the U. On day one of the course, Alison had chosen to sit center-left at the corner junction where one long end of a rectangle met the short side. She stayed there all week, departing her chair at the end of each class session and then reclaiming it the following day. Alison took learning seriously. She was invested.

I pressed play and the opening credits began to roll. Alison must have sensed what was about to happen. Even before the main footage began, she suddenly slid her chair out from the table, grabbed her bag, and quietly walked out of the classroom. The other students in the lecture hall remained, staring at the screen. I'm not sure any of them noticed. But from where I was situated, Alison's sudden departure made an impression. The reel continued playing, and the students looked on. As discreetly as possible, I made my way to the side of the room and exited. The clip runs approximately four minutes, and I figured I had enough time to check in on Alison before returning to lead a discussion. When I stepped into the hallway, Alison was standing several feet down the corridor. We stared at each other for a moment, and then I carefully approached her. A young woman in her mid-twenties, Alison certainly had the right to excuse herself from watching the commercial if she felt that it was too triggering or painful to view. I wanted to check in without being intrusive. And so, in what I hoped was a polite, respectful manner, I asked her, "Is everything okay?"

"I just can't watch this right now."

"Okay." I paused for a moment, caught between a will to understand and a respect for her boundaries and privacy. "You can take whatever time you need. I'm going to head back in and discuss the commercial with the group. Whenever you're ready, you're free to rejoin us."

Alison looked at me and nodded. I could see she was shaking.

Quietly, I returned to the lecture hall, just in time for the cars to collide and the ad to finish. I then facilitated a group discussion on the commercial. At some point during that discussion—I don't remember precisely when—Alison reentered the classroom and returned to her seat. We completed that day and the remainder of the course as well. The incident was not mentioned again . . . until it was.

On Friday evening, July 24th, I was sitting in my Brooklyn apartment, recovering from thirty-five hours of graduate-level instruction. It was sometime after 8 p.m. Netflix. Chinese food. A cold beer. As I surfed new releases, an email came through. It was from Alison.

> Regarding the "It Can Wait" commercial, I just wanted to explain before I forgot to do so that the commercial was a trigger for me because of my experiences with car crashes. My father was in a terrible car crash when I was in high school. . . . That person hit a car that flipped over, then the car that flipped over and crushed my father's car. He is fine now. I didn't really drive until I was 22 because I had so many fears about driving.
>
> Then I had a bad car accident in October because I fainted while I was driving. . . . I blacked out as I was steering toward the telephone pole and applying the brakes. I woke up on impact and because of the sound of the crash . . .
>
> The commercial just brought up a lot of the fears and guilt I have about continuing to drive knowing that I have now fainted while driving . . . If I ever faint again while driving, though, I would lose my license. The commercial just was hard to process at this point in time. (July 24, 2015)

Most of the time, we don't know what our students are thinking. They show up to class or don't. They raise their hands to contribute or don't. They write their papers or don't. In some ways, what we see in them and what we get to know is somewhat superficial. Like a curator who chooses the paintings in a gallery, each student carefully selects the parts of themselves they want to exhibit in class. We know what they let us know; we hypothesize the rest.

Shakespeare has a line about this in *Macbeth*: "There is no art to find the mind's construction in the face" (1.4.13). Jennifer is wide-eyed and optimistic. She takes exceptional notes and talks excitedly about James Baldwin and Emily Dickinson. Jake, on the other hand, appears distracted. He's missing multiple assignments and often socializes when he should be focused. The one is the model student; the other is on a road to nowhere. But these are our assumptions—full of sound and fury, often signifying nothing. As Phillip Roth writes in *American Pastoral*:

> You get them wrong before you meet them, while you're anticipating meeting them; you get them wrong while you're with them; and then you go home to tell somebody else about the meeting and you get them all wrong again. . . . It's getting them wrong that is living, getting them wrong and wrong and wrong and then, on careful reconsideration, getting them wrong again. That's how we know we're alive: we're wrong. (Roth, 2016, 35)

We get our students wrong all the time. Despite our best powers of intuition, we don't know why Jennifer thrives while Jake struggles. Maybe Jennifer's parents have taught her how to play the role of the model student. She believes an A and an acceptance letter from Cornell is her way to earn daddy's love. Underneath the perfect student is an anxious, depressed teenager who just wants dad to accept her for who she is. Perhaps Jake is much more engaged than we suspect; he's just doing it his way. He hasn't told us, but this is the first time in his life that he's enjoying reading and writing. During his free time, Jake's reading *Catcher in the Rye* and beginning to figure out who he really is. At the end of the year, we'll be surprised when he writes us a note saying that our course changed the way he thinks about the world.

When Alison left the classroom on July 21st, I was reminded of how little we know about the lives of the students in our classrooms. For fourteen of them, the AT&T commercial led to a rich discussion on narrative compression and storytelling. For Alison, it tapped into a network within her psychology that was shattered, fragile, and overwhelmed. She had followed up her departure with an email explaining why she had been triggered. What was the next move? Did she want to talk more about it? Was I supposed to follow up by suggesting a meeting or a phone call? Or would a simple email suffice, thanking her for letting me know and wishing her well going forward? In all honesty, I didn't know. I couldn't tell whether this was the beginning of a new phase in our relationship or the declaration of its termination. The course was over. She'd head back to New Jersey and resume her teaching career in the fall. I'd wrap up final grades and take August off before resuming my doctoral work in September.

What I did know was that I respected Alison. I respected her for having the wherewithal to walk out of the room when she felt overwhelmed, and then I respected her more for having the courage to reach out to me at the conclusion of our work. She could have simply sat there, rattled, while the commercial played. She could have gritted her teeth and gripped the bottom of her chair, holding on while the tempest raged within. But she didn't. She exercised her agency and right to prioritize her own mental health in the face of an overwhelming and disarming educational experience. Many students, overcome by shame, guilt, and denial (van der Kolk, 2015; Herman, 1992) don't know how to do that.

July 21 was an important day in my history as an English teacher. On the day Alison chose to step outside of my classroom, it was the first time in fifteen years of teaching that I can recall an individual leaving the room because the material felt too intense or too personally triggering. It's very likely it had happened before, but I hadn't noticed. And never had a student reached out directly to explain that something I had done had tapped into their personal traumas in a way that felt destabilizing and devastating.

But in July of 2015, the concept of the trigger warning had been getting considerable press. Popular media outlets such as *The Atlantic*, Vox, and *The New York Times* were publishing strong, opinionated pieces either advocating for or condemning its usage. Greg Lukianoff and Jonathan Haidt had recently written a scathing critique of trigger warnings, *The Coddling of the American Mind*, in which they had blamed progressive, liberal arts colleges for pandering to the capricious fragilities of hyper-liberal, "woke" students. Kate Manne, a philosophy professor at Cornell University, had fired back in her *Times* article, "Why I Use Trigger Warnings." Manne forcefully argued that trigger warnings enhance, rather than shut down, deep engagement with triggering content.

And now there was a very real scenario that had taken place in my classroom. I hadn't provided the students with a trigger warning. If I had, would Alison have left the room anyway? In the wake of July 21st, I began to think more conscientiously about the issue of student trauma, about how our curricular aims can unwittingly destabilize or unsettle students who have experienced traumas that mirror elements of the content we teach. I began to think about this complicated duality: literature, by its very nature, is often a reservoir for the selfsame traumas that shatter the lives of some of our students. Hamlet contemplates suicide. Blanche is raped. Westover suffers from child abuse and religious persecution. Many of our students face the same realities at home. And for those students, will reading literature retraumatize them? Or will student survivors feel relieved to read about others who endure similar hardships? Might the pages we read provide comfort and validation for troubling aspects of their lives?

I began to consider literature more holistically—not only the books we build into a high school or post-secondary curriculum but even many of the books we grow up reading—even the books I read aloud to my six- and eight-year-old children. *Charlotte's Web. Where the Wild Things Are. The Lion, the Witch and the Wardrobe.* The Harry Potter books. Charlotte dies. Max contends with monsters. Edmund gets seduced by the White Witch. Harry must ultimately overcome Voldemort. On almost a definitional level, literature, like the life it seeks to capture, is replete with trauma. Alison's car crash. Windsor's preoccupation with the abusive man. They were two versions of the same phenomenon. And it was fifteen years later, and still the best path forward wasn't clear. Those vehicles in the AT&T spot had not been the only things crashing into each other on that sweltering July afternoon.

For the rest of that summer and into the following fall, what happened with Alison Scott at Columbia University set into motion a cascade of thoughts that gripped my mind for some time. Those thoughts centered around student trauma and what it means to teach literature that might trigger the trauma histories of my students. One part of me interpreted Alison's email as an apologetic explanation for why she had left the room. Another part of me wondered whether she was blaming me: *If you knew that the AT&T commercial contained potentially triggering content, then why hadn't you given us a trigger warning?*

Or maybe she was doing both. Regardless, the wormwood of navigating trauma in the English classroom began to gnaw at my consciousness. I began to ruminate on whether I should have provided a trigger warning for the AT&T car crash. More broadly, I began to wonder whether trigger warnings should be utilized in advance of all dramatic scenes in the English classroom—when Tom strikes Myrtle and breaks her nose (*The Great Gatsby*), when Oedipus kills his father, when Alison Bechdel's dad commits suicide (*Fun Home*), when One-Fifteen shoots Khalil (*The Hate U Give*)? The list goes on and on and on.

As an English teacher, did my allegiance lie with the authors I teach or with the students in my class? Or with both? Does literature featuring complex trauma play a therapeutic role for student survivors, or does it have the potential to retraumatize? The course was over. I had seven weeks of freedom heading into the fall of 2015. An invitation to spend a weekend on the Cape. Some light summer reading. A pool party or two. But my mind began to burn. I couldn't get Alison's email out of my head . . .

Down the Rabbit Hole: Unpacking Trauma

For the next two and a half years, I took a deep dive into trauma: van der Kolk's *The Body Keeps the Score*, Judith Herman's *Trauma and Recovery*, Elizabeth Dutro's *The Vulnerable Heart of Literacy: Centering Trauma as Powerful Pedagogy.* These and other texts became the bedfellows of my unquiet mind. I had concentrated in English literature as an undergraduate at Harvard. I had studied pedagogy during my doctoral program at Teachers College, but, like many English teachers, I had never learned specifically about trauma. And so it suddenly dawned on me that the only way to better understand what had happened with Alison Scott—and fifteen years earlier with Windsor—was to immerse myself in what happens to student survivors who have endured traumatic experiences. The trigger warning, whether I used it or chose not to use it, was a type of intervention. But I didn't just want to stop at the intervention; I wanted to understand the wound.

A Reminder: What Is Trauma?

Trauma, by its very nature, impacts the survivor in a number of complex, unpredictable, and destabilizing ways (Levine, 2010; Stolorow, 2007; Carello and Butler, 2014). Some traumas are overt and dramatic in nature—violent attacks, sexual assaults, car crashes, racial injustices. These constitute the big T traumas I referred to in chapter 1 (Howell and Itzkowitz, 2016). Big T traumas often fall under the umbrella of what we call impact trauma: events that clearly elicit significant adverse responses in the survivor. Alison's car crash and the sudden death of Yana's father fall into the category of big T, impact traumas. But traumas are not always obvious. For every Alison, Yana, or Elizabeth Dutro, there will be students who endure traumas without necessarily knowing they are being traumatized. Slights, rejection, neglect, estrangement—these can penetrate the psyche and wear away at an individual's tolerance and self-esteem.

A number of our students will endure *relational trauma,* which typically consists of small traumas that present a persistent disruption to the child's sense of feeling safe and loved within the nuclear family. Still others will suffer from what Mark Epstein refers to as the trauma of everyday life (Epstein, 2014): struggling to find a suitable social group, falling behind in class, lacking money relative to classmates. These small traumas become additive over time and have a cumulative impact on an individual's sense of well-being and self-esteem. Both big T and little t traumas can have profound impacts on the brains and bodies of survivors (van der Kolk, 2015). And since no two traumas or individual survivors are identical, traumatic events tend to impact each individual in ways that are specific to the particular personality, life circumstances, and survival mechanisms of the student at hand.

Marsha: Trauma and the Brain

If you'll indulge me for the next few pages, I'd like to take some time to illustrate how trauma can impact the brain. When I first learned about this as a doctoral student preparing for my dissertation, it completely transformed my understanding of traumatized students. Though much of it is rooted in neuroscience, I found it powerfully relevant to the English classroom. My hope is that by imparting some trauma neuroscience to you (Kristen will do more of this in chapter 9), I can help to provide a deeper understanding of what it means for students when they get triggered by curricular content that taps into traumatic feelings and memories.

In recent years, it has become increasingly clear that trauma rewires the brain. According to Harvard psychiatrist and trauma expert Bessel van der Kolk, trauma results in a recalibration of the brain and nervous system:

> Research from these new disciplines has revealed that trauma produces actual physiological changes, including a recalibration of the brain's alarm system, an increase in stress hormone activity, and alterations in the system that filters relevant information from irrelevant. (van der Kolk, 2014, 2–3)

When I first read *The Body Keeps the Score* in the fall of 2015, I was both fascinated and stunned by the tremendous impact trauma has on brain development and neurological functioning. Bessel van der Kolk's remarkable insights helped to illuminate the type of responses that might be occurring in my student survivors when their traumas were triggered. Since my initial interest in trauma had been spurred by my interaction with Alison, I became particularly drawn to a story that van der Kolk relays about one of his patients, Marsha, who suffers a horrific car crash.

Prior to the accident, Marsha was a forty-two-year-old schoolteacher. Thirteen years before meeting van der Kolk, Marsha, pregnant at the time, was driving her five-year-old daughter to an outing when she accidentally ran a red light. Her car was sideswiped by an oncoming vehicle, killing her five-year-old daughter instantly. Shortly thereafter, Marsha's unborn baby died as well. Not surprisingly, this horrific event devastated Marsha, shattering her faith and significantly redirecting the course of her life: "overnight she had changed from a cheerful woman who was the life of the party to a haunted and depressed person filled with self-blame" (41). In terms of her professional life as an educator, Marsha could no longer stand to be around schoolchildren; she moved out of the classroom and into administration.

Evidence of the neurological impact to Marsha's brain manifested itself when van der Kolk enrolled her in a research study. Using a PET scan (a functional imaging tool designed to study blood flow in the brain), van der Kolk observed Marsha's brain. Marsha was instructed to produce a trauma script that re-created the day of the accident. She also was instructed to describe a scenario where she felt safe and in control: "One person described her morning routine; another, sitting on the porch of a farmhouse in Vermont overlooking the hills" (40). The narratives were converted into audio recordings. While Marsha lay in the scanner, she listened to the recordings. For Alison, the trauma script might have read something like this:

> *It's a Wednesday afternoon. You are driving along 95 South headed to your client in Bergen County. You're listening to Bob Seger through the Bluetooth audio as*

you take exit 17. Suddenly, you begin to feel faint, sweat beads on your forehead, and you find that you are losing your balance. You grip tighter to the steering wheel, fearing that you are about to faint. There is a bag of pretzels and a bottle of Poland Spring water to your right. You reach for it, and place a handful of pretzels into your mouth. You have a sip of water, but your throat is getting dry and tight. You're beginning to see floaters, and your vision is getting blurry. Realizing that you are about to pass out, you quickly look for a place to turn off the road. Up ahead you see an open area where you can park your car. You begin to turn the wheel, but then suddenly everything goes dark. A screech, a sudden thrust of the wheel, and then a loud CRASH. You start from the black haze. The airbags have released, and you are sitting in your vehicle, disoriented. The front of your car is wrapped around a telephone pole, and you are struggling to catch your breath. Your meeting with your clients is in fifteen minutes, and you know you won't make it. You sit in terrified fear, unable to move.

And though we do not have Alison's PET scans to show us how her brain reacted on July 21, we might be able to hypothesize what she experienced by examining van der Kolk's PET scans on Marsha. As Marsha listened to the car crash, one similar to the one that killed her children, her brain and body ramped up into physiological arousal: "her heart rate started to race and her blood pressure jumped" (41). The images from Marsha's PET scan are featured below:

Figure 2.1: PET Scan Images Highlighting Trauma's Effect on the Brain

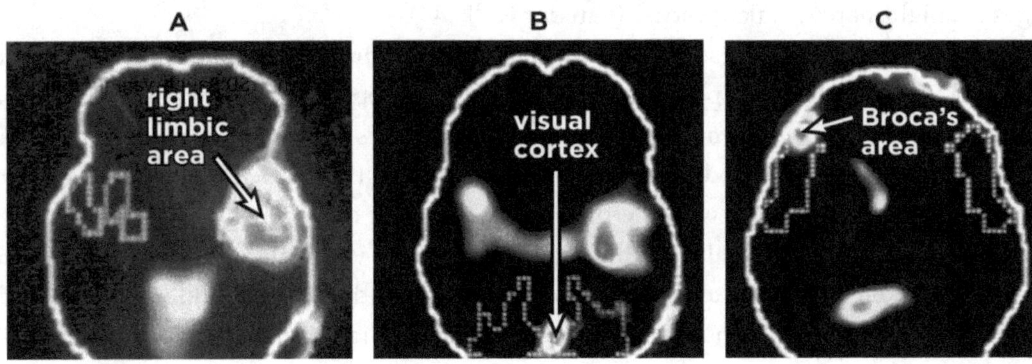

Image A highlights a hyper-concentration of oxygen in the right limbic area of the brain. Increased concentrations of oxygen in a brain region indicate that this neurological region is hyperactive with excess oxygen required to sustain neurological activity. And why the right limbic area? The right limbic area is the house of the amygdala, an emotional region of the brain. Humans rely on the amygdala to "warn us of impending danger and to activate the body's stress response" (42). While absorbing her trauma script, Marsha's brain was flooded with memories of her traumatic experience. It ramped up into fight or flight, reliving the trauma in the present tense even though the crash had occurred thirteen years earlier. As I will discuss in more detail in chapter 5, sympathetic, fight-or-flight responses are typical when survivors get triggered (Levine, 2010). Perhaps this had been the way Alison Scott felt on that July afternoon in 2015, sitting in my teaching of drama class, recalling what it had felt like to faint at the wheel and crash into a telephone pole?

Image C highlights something very important as well: "(o)ur most surprising finding was a white spot in the left frontal lobe of the cortex, in a region called Broca's area" (45). If the amygdala became hyperactivated, then Broca's region essentially shut down: "Without a functioning Broca's area, you cannot put your thoughts and feelings into words. Our scans showed that Broca's area went offline whenever a flashback was triggered" (43). Shakespeare captures a breaking down of Broca's region in Macbeth after Duncan's body is discovered. Macduff enters, exclaiming: "Oh horror! horror! horror! Tongue nor heart cannot conceive nor name thee! . . . Confusion now hath made thee a masterpiece!" (II.iii.72–75).

Bessel van der Kolk argues that all trauma is preverbal. Traumatized individuals often howl in pain, call for their mothers, refuse to speak, and lose the capacity to verbalize. Becoming mute is a predictable response to powerfully overwhelming experiences that inundate and shatter the individual (Herman, 1992; Levine, 2010). Years or even decades after suffering a traumatic event, survivors often have difficulty finding words for what has happened to them. The failure of words that results from traumatic experience often engenders "haunting images . . . nightmares . . . flashbacks" (van der Kolk, 44).

Finally, van der Kolk's research team noticed that Brodmann's area (Image B, contained within the visual cortex) lit up when Marsha listened to her trauma script. Under normal, homeostatic conditions, Brodmann's area distributes images to various regions of the brain. But for trauma survivors, Brodmann's area often clings to traumatic memories. In essence, the visual memory associated with the trauma gets trapped or frozen, codified in its original weight and intensity. As she lay in the scanner, thirteen years after the original trauma, Marsha was taken right back to the car crash. Her brain and body responded as though the accident were happening in the present tense. Part of her brain remained frozen in the past; the trauma continued.

How Neuroscience Can Help Us Understand How Trauma Impacts Students in Our Classrooms

Understanding how trauma impacts the brain can offer valuable lessons to English teachers struggling to understand student survivors. When our students get triggered, their brains can take over, causing both physiological and psychological responses that interfere significantly with our attempts at engaging them in deep reading (Sullivan, Tinberg, and Blau, 2017) and aesthetic interaction (Rosenblatt, 1938; Vinz and Pindyck, 2022). When we push to activate rich, immersive engagement, their traumas may push back. And because trauma often has the effect of making the survivor feel like their traumas are recurring in the present tense, the type of reading we see as essential in the classroom may make them feel too vulnerable and too psychologically threatened. And this may help to explain why Alison Scott needed to physically get up and leave the room. Even though on some objective level, there was no real harm or threat in that classroom at Columbia University, Alison's mind interpreted the space as dangerous, causing her to flee for safety and seek self-preservation.

As I mentioned in chapter 1, something similar happened to Elizabeth Dutro when she was a sixteen-year-old high school junior:

> I was 16, sitting in junior English, when my teacher, with her usual style and drama began reading the first lines of Karl Shapiro's poem about sudden trauma, the tragedy of innocent lives cut short. I heard the word ambulance; I saw it on the page in front of me, the stark black print beginning to waver, along with the words that followed—stretchers, mangled, hospital. A slight tremble in my fingers spread quickly to more general quaking. Just a few lines of verse and I was unable to hold my pencil, unable to focus on the page or my classmates' faces, each blurring into the other. At the poem's ninth line I bolted from the classroom, unsure how I had managed to will my trembling limbs to move, and only slightly aware of the pause in my teacher's reading. I ran, to some deserted locker-lined corridor, to escape the words that had too soon spoken my experience back to me. (Dutro, 2008, 423)

When our students have survived significant traumas, they may not be able to tolerate some of the curricular choices we make. They may need to prioritize their mental health and emotional safety over fully immersing themselves in the work. Although we might hope they can engage in deep reading (Sullivan, Tinberg, and Blau, 2017), transact aesthetically (Rosenblatt, 1938), and be the book (Wilhelm, 1997), it's important we understand that sometimes they simply can't. The type of emotional vulnerability and resilience ideal for rich, immersive engagement with literature may require a psychological readiness that breaks down or shatters in the face of acute traumatic experience (Dutro, 2008; Carello and Butler, 2014).

As English teachers, we need to be mindful of this reality, at times shelving some of the emphasis we place on academic rigor in favor of a teaching approach that more deeply considers and accounts for the type of student fragility that inevitably results from trauma (Dutro, 2008; Carello and Butler, 2014). As sensitive and deliberate as we often are when we attend to authors' careful creation of words, narrative, symbols, and motif, there will be times when we need to be equally sensitive to the limitations that our students express (either overtly or unintentionally) in the face of curricular encounters that feel too destabilizing, overwhelming, and threatening. Somewhere between the therapist and the traditional English teacher is a version of ourselves, an educator who is highly empathic, conscientious, and therapeutic, somebody who is able to know when being caring is more important than offering correction (chapter 4); somebody who senses when it's more important to take a break than to push forward (chapter 7); somebody who can listen and hear the student's need but also know we will likely not be the right person to try to fix, repair, or undo what has been done (chapter 8).

When Alison walked out of my classroom on July 21st of 2015, and then when she followed up that departure with an email explanation a few days later, I think she was looking to be heard. She was asking me to listen to her, and she wanted to know that I wasn't going to punish or alienate her for the choice she made. In the traditional power dynamic that exists in almost any classroom (Butler, 1995; Britzman and Pitt, 2004), students often feel subservient and indebted to their teachers in a way that is at times old-fashioned, problematic, and arbitrary. But when it comes to trauma and the psychological vulnerabilities that result from it, sometimes it is more important for the student to be the one who can take control of their environment and do what they feel they need to do to regain a sense of safety and comfort. As English teachers, if we resist this power inversion or prioritize our own need for authority and control, we may unwittingly retraumatize the student.

When I look back at that summer afternoon in my classroom at Columbia University, I don't see Alison as somebody who was being manipulative, avoidant, or disengaged. I see a person who became overwhelmed because the content hit too close to home for her. In a fight-or-flight moment, she reflexively rose from her seat and bolted the room. It wasn't premeditated, it wasn't deliberate, and it certainly wasn't an act of defiance. It was a traumatic response from somebody who had endured a terrifying trauma.

On Friday, July 24th, after she'd had a few days to process what had occurred, she reached out to me in a far more deliberate manner and explained, to the best of her knowledge, why she had left the room. Bear in mind, she had no obligation to do so. I would not have penalized her had she not explained. For as little as I understood the exact circumstances surrounding Alison's departure, I did understand well enough that she had left because she felt like she needed to leave—and that was enough for me. No problem. No worries. No penalty. Understood. You do what you need to do in order to feel safe. If the demands of the moment are too personally devastating, alarming, or destabilizing, I don't want you to feel pressured to fulfill the requirements of my curriculum. I'm okay if you sometimes need to prioritize yourself.

That week in July, Alison didn't need me to teach her about drama and literature; she needed me to hear, accept, and understand her without being punitive, judgmental, or critical. When we can learn to put aside our personal hubris, when we can realize that our curricular aims, insistence on authority, and need for control are at times less significant than the psychological needs of our students, then we may begin to act as therapeutic English teachers who run classrooms that are both pedagogically sound and trauma informed.

Chapter 2: Questions for Reflection

1. Knowing what you know about the content of the AT&T commercial, would you have provided a trigger warning?
2. If I had provided a trigger warning, do you think the outcome might have been different?
3. Imagine that Alison has walked out of your classroom. You go out into the hallway to check on her. How do you assess the situation? What clues do you look for in her? What do you say or not say? How do you navigate her wish for privacy with your moral obligation to her as a student and a member of the educational community?
4. Imagine you are me on the night of July 24th. You receive Alison's email explaining her history of car crashes. Write the email you send back to her.
5. Today, almost a decade later, what do you think Alison sees when she looks back at what happened on July 21st of 2015?

3

Why the Trigger Warning Simply Isn't Enough

In recent years, the trigger warning has been proposed as a type of solution to the highly complex and nuanced problem of student trauma in the English classroom. But the research is fairly muddy: trigger warnings may not protect students from being triggered. They may even induce anxiety and heighten the triggered response. In this chapter, I (Adam Wolfsdorf) will seek to broaden the conversation, moving the discourse away from the trigger warning and into more comprehensive ways of looking at and handling student traumatic response.

i touched her in the middle of her heart.
i never saw her again.
—Nayyirah Waheed, *Sting*

Right around the time that Alison Scott got up and left my classroom, conversations about trigger warnings had taken center stage nationally. As a growing awareness of mental health and student psychological well-being advanced in the popular media (Vox, *The Atlantic*, *The New York Times*), trigger warnings were being promoted by some as a remedy of sorts to the burgeoning problem at hand—as a tool educators could utilize to protect students from the potential discomfort and triggering impacts of confronting classroom content that too closely aligned with unsettling personal traumas. Alison herself had sent me an email wondering why I had not included a trigger warning in advance of airing the AT&T ad. With all the buzz circulating within the media, and with pressures relevant to protecting student psychological fragility mounting within the academy, I decided that it was time to wrestle with the question: *Are trigger warnings the solution?*

It would be wonderfully convenient if trigger warnings were enough, if including a content warning prior to teaching potentially unsettling material could do the comprehensive work of helping students feel comfortable, safe, and accounted for in classrooms. Unfortunately, they don't. Like Marsha, who was keenly aware of the trauma script she was about to hear (after all, she had created it herself), trauma survivors respond to triggering content even when they know what is about to happen. As a show of respect or perhaps because we don't know what else to do, we might provide a content warning, hoping that doing so may ease the anxiety of the potential interaction and make the learning experience feel safer and more palatable. And it is easy to understand why many teachers believe trigger warnings are important. After all, trauma is a serious business, and we want to do everything within our power to make our classrooms feel safe, compassionate, and welcoming. That said, the data on trigger warnings may run anathema to our best intentions: despite what we hope, forewarning of potentially traumatic content may not prevent the survivor from getting psychologically triggered. In fact, providing trigger warnings may trigger students even more. A recent research study out of Harvard University (Jones, Bellet, and McNally, 2020) suggests that using trigger warnings intensified anxiety among survivors:

> Bellet, Jones, and McNally (2018) . . . found that trigger warnings undermined participants' sense of their resilience to potential future traumatic events and their sense of the resilience of others. They also reported a moderation effect—among individuals who believed that words were emotionally harmful, trigger warnings acutely increased anxiety reactions. (Jones, Bellet, and McNally, 2020, 906)

In some ways, the trigger warning may be fueled by what Fitzgerald refers to in *The Great Gatsby* as "infinite hope" (2). Teachers who provide warnings may believe they will facilitate classroom discourse, protect the psychological fragilities of trauma survivors, and engender bold spaces for rigorous academic encounters with complex content. Kate Manne, for instance, an associate professor of philosophy at Cornell University, published a *New York Times* piece arguing that trigger warnings facilitate engagement by helping survivors to psychologically prepare themselves for encounters with potentially triggering content:

> Increasingly, professors like me simply give students notice in their syllabuses, or before certain reading assignments. The point is not to enable—let alone encourage—students to skip these readings or our subsequent class discussion (both of which are mandatory in my courses, absent a formal exemption). Rather, it is to allow those who are sensitive to these subjects to prepare themselves for reading about them, and better

> manage their reactions. The evidence suggests that at least some of the students in any given class of mine are likely to have suffered some sort of trauma, whether from sexual assault or another type of abuse or violence. So I think the benefits of trigger warnings can be significant. (2015)

And Manne has a valuable point: as educators, we have a responsibility to all our students to create conditions that invite rich, aesthetic engagement. Yet if we recall the neuroscience evidence from the previous chapter (I'm referring specifically to Marsha's PET scan), we begin to recognize that no matter what we hope to achieve through utilizing trigger warnings—whether we endorse, reject, or feel downright ambivalent about them—the science is unambiguous: they do not prevent students from getting triggered. In this regard, the trigger warning alone is not sufficient or comprehensive enough to protect students from encounters with triggering content. So, regardless of what we want or wish, it is important that we shelve our ideologies for a moment and pay close attention to the science, considering what it can teach us about attending to the trauma responses of our student survivors.

One thing that trigger warnings fail to account for is how messy and overwhelming trauma can be. I have made the case in previous publications that putting a trigger warning before a potentially triggering curricular event is a bit like laying a Band-Aid over a geyser (Wolfsdorf, 2019, 2020). As Judith Herman describes in *Trauma and Recovery*:

> At the moment of trauma, the victim is rendered helpless by overwhelming force. . . . Traumatic events overwhelm the ordinary systems of care that give people a sense of control, connection, and meaning. . . . Traumatic events are extraordinary, not because they occur rarely, but rather because they overwhelm the ordinary human adaptations to life. . . . They confront human beings with the extremities of helplessness and terror, and evoke the responses of catastrophe. (Herman, 1992, 33)

When it gets activated, the sheer power and the untamable energy of traumatic response can overwhelm cognition. In a process called *hemispheric polarization*, the left brain goes offline (van der Kolk, 2014), leaving the survivor susceptible to right-brain responses that are emotional, dramatic, and tactile without the balance afforded by the left brain's logic, sequencing, and linearity. This disconnect between left and right brain leads to a breakdown in executive functioning, which is a hallmark feature of traumatic response (Levine & Mate, 2010). The cumulative psychological impact of being triggered is simply too strong; the trigger warning is not sufficient to mitigate the triggered effect. In this sense, though the trigger warning may seem like the solution, in actuality it might do more to calm the helplessness of the educator than to ease the potential response of the trauma survivor, who carries the burden of their experience into the classroom. And this is to say nothing of the fact that trigger warnings may unwittingly encourage avoidance, which actually can damage the student and erode that student's resilience. McNally writes: "trigger warnings are counter-therapeutic because they encourage avoidance of reminders of trauma, and avoidance maintains PTSD" (McNally, 2016). The brain is delicate, subtle, and intuitive. As might occur when a doctor tells you not to get worried when she takes your blood pressure, the very act of forewarning can compel blood to flow with more pressure. There has to be a better solution.

So if they aren't the answer—if, in fact, trigger warnings can be anathema to the type of teaching an English teacher prioritizes when they set out to enculturate classroom spaces that induce aesthetic, engaged responses (Greene, 1988; Rosenblatt, 1938)—then why has it come about in the first place, and why do so many English teachers hold out hope that it will solve the problem? Perhaps the answer is complicated? Or maybe it's simpler than we think: teachers often don't know what else to do.

Why Our Students Are Getting So Triggered

From Vladimir Putin and Tucker Carlson to COVID-19, social media, global warming, school shootings, and George Floyd, America and the myth of the American ideal currently sway in the balance like the branches of Kafka's tree. From the 2016 election of Donald Trump to mask mandates, TikTok, ventilators, and vaccine hesitancy, the long curtain that once separated the common American citizen from the man in the Emerald Palace has been torn down. And the man playing the role of Oz is now right there, no longer a bold, all-powerful demigod but instead an awkward, bumbling old man doing his best to pull the right levers and keep the masses in check. The tearing apart of the American ideal—which perhaps was initiated in the twenty-first century when two planes smashed into the World Trade Centers and then accelerated with the advent of social media—has demolished certain psychological supports that for centuries served to provide foundational stability and structure to the American psyche. As these psychological pillars have toppled, a dark underbelly of greed, corruption, and godlessness has risen from the Valley of Ashes, creating a societal insecurity and jitteriness that deeply impacts, among other things, today's youth.

In recent years, depression and anxiety rates among school-aged children have skyrocketed. According to statistics from the CDC, six million school-aged children have been diagnosed with ADHD, one in ten suffers from anxiety, and another three million battle depression[iv] (Bitsko et al., 2022). These numbers are burgeoning over time. For children ages six to seventeen, depression and anxiety rates increased from 5.4 percent in 2003 to 8 percent in 2007 and to 8.4 percent in 2011 (Bitsko et al., 2022). In 2018–2019, among adolescents aged twelve to seventeen:

- 15.1 percent had a major depressive episode.
- 36.7 percent had persistent feelings of sadness or hopelessness.
- 4.1 percent had a substance use disorder.
- 18.8 percent seriously considered attempting suicide.
- 15.7 percent made a suicide plan.
- 8.9 percent attempted suicide.
- 2.5 percent made a suicide attempt requiring medical treatment. (Bitsko et al., 2022)

Mental health scholars from BJ Casey and Peter Blos to Jess Shatkin and Alexa Curtis have noted the extraordinary challenges endemic to adolescence[v]: self-esteem and body image, cyber addiction, underage sex, teen pregnancy, bullying, stress, and peer pressure.

What gets glamorized on shows like Euphoria becomes far more complicated in the classroom. With the penetration of social media (Lukianoff and Haidt, 2015) and the ever-accelerating speed of technology (Friedman, 2016), the instabilities and challenges endemic to the adolescent experiences of our students have become magnified and intensified. Although there have always been inequities, wealth and access gaps, and media influence, the rapid acceleration and intensification of these forces may be compelling our students to seek an extra layer of protection, comfort, and security. When they arrive in our classrooms, their personal instabilities may be competing more viscerally with our curricular aims. #metoo, BLM, LGBTQ+, Action for the Climate Emergency, Russia/Ukraine, and a global pandemic . . . these only add to the general feelings of instability, unease, and dissatisfaction that many current adolescents navigate daily. With the incredible proliferation and accessibility of content, we are living during a time of intense disquietude. Desirable colleges have become more expensive and increasingly difficult to get into; parents have been forced to work longer hours to make ends meet, and inflation has driven up home prices, all but abolishing (for many) the attainability of the American dream.

The gross instability affecting students' emotional wellness has compelled many adolescents to seek additional support from the adults who educate them. The trigger warning, in this regard, may be less about what it actually remedies and more a symptom of a student's wish to feel taken care of and protected from a battering world that is changing too quickly and moving too fast. English teachers who provide trigger warnings might be seen as more conscientious, thoughtful, and empathetic, whereas those who choose not to may be vilified as being careless, callous, or disconnected. But when it comes down to attending to the needs of traumatized students, boiling things down to a black-and-white, all-or-nothing exultation or condemnation based on trigger warning use seems to miss the boat. The trauma is the issue, not the trigger warning. How trauma-informed English teachers handle the complexities attendant to student trauma seems much more important than whether Ms. Cabeje or Dr. Thomason lets the class know in advance that Tom is about to strike Myrtle. Our student survivors want to know that we see them, that we have some awareness of their pain, and that we can promote and do our best to produce classroom environments where they feel safe enough to feel what they feel, even when the feelings brought up by a text become intense and penetrating (Dutro, 2008; Felman and Laub, 1992).

Whether we provide trigger warnings or choose not to provide trigger warnings, our students *will* get triggered. In some ways, the real issue at hand is not about prevention of uncomfortable feelings; a good English classroom will spur uncomfortable feelings and produce uncomfortable conversations. The more important consideration is what we do when our students do get triggered. Have we relayed to them that if things feel too intense, they are welcome to step out of the classroom? Have we done the essential work of letting our students know we will be teaching a number of complex narratives that will at times be disturbing, disquieting, and even, dare I say, triggering? Have we addressed the class and let them know they should feel free to reach out or touch base if they feel intensely triggered by a literary encounter that viscerally destabilizes them? Have we worked in alternative texts that students can choose to read in the event that they find a particular book, poem, play, or short story too disturbing? In my estimation, the fallacy of the trigger warning has always centered around the idea that it will somehow prevent or reduce the number of students who get triggered in the English classroom. If texts are doing their job, then students will feel their power. And should the English teacher be so concerned about protecting the emotional safety of their students that they will likely foster English classrooms that are too sanitized and anesthetic, which runs against the goals set down by our most celebrated practitioners (Dewey, Greene, Vinz, Morrell, Blau, Rosenblatt, and Moffett). As J. K. Rowling stated in June of 2008 to a class of graduating seniors at Harvard:

> Some failure in life is inevitable. It is impossible to live without failing at something, unless you live so cautiously that you might as well not have lived at all—in which case, you fail by default.

We do not fail our students if we trigger them. We did not create their traumas, and we are not their therapists. We do fail them if we sanitize our classrooms so thoroughly that brave, emotionally rich reading and writing opportunities become discouraged and taboo. We also fail them if they get triggered by a curricular choice, and we don't take the time to check in with them, hear them, empathetically support them. On some paradoxical level, it may be the case that the survivor who gets triggered in our presence may trust us enough to feel their feelings in our classrooms. Maybe they are not able to feel them in the presence of their parents, or with other teachers, or with their friends. As can happen among patients who peel away their defenses in the presence of their therapists, maybe something we are doing in the classroom has provided a cultural environment where they feel safe and secure enough to be triggered in the first place.

A few weeks ago, I was teaching Shakespeare's Sonnet 73 to a group of first-year students.

That time of year thou mayst in me behold
When yellow leaves, or none, or few, do hang
Upon those boughs which shake against the cold,
Bare ruin'd choirs, where late the sweet birds sang.
In me thou see'st the twilight of such day
As after sunset fadeth in the west,
Which by and by black night doth take away,
Death's second self, that seals up all in rest.
In me thou see'st the glowing of such fire
That on the ashes of his youth doth lie,
As the death-bed whereon it must expire,
Consum'd with that which it was nourish'd by.
This thou perceiv'st, which makes thy love more strong,
To love that well which thou must leave ere long.

Using an inquiry method I learned from Sheridan Blau when I was a doctoral student at Teachers College (Blau, 2003), I asked the students to:

i) Read the sonnet.
ii) Underline the words, phrases, or moments that resonated for them.
iii) Write down 2–3 questions they have about the sonnet.
iv) Write a one-paragraph analysis explaining what they think Shakespeare is expressing in the poem.
v) Rate their understanding of the poem on a scale from 1–100.

I gave the students seven minutes to work through the method. At the conclusion of seven minutes, we read through the sonnet together. I divided it up into four sections (quatrains one, two, three, and the final couplet) and asked for volunteers to read each part. Following the read-aloud, we discussed the poem as a group, first doing a line-by-line translation and then pulling back the lens to look more broadly at Shakespeare's intention.

As tends to happen most of the time when I teach this poem, the students began to see that the sonnet is focused on loss and how the reality of loss can intensify the love that we feel for somebody: "This thou perceiv'st, which makes thy love more strong,/To love that well which thou must leave ere long." (I was actually asked to recite this poem at the funeral of my former Teachers College professor John Browne, who passed away from lymphoma in 2017.)

At the conclusion of the class, as students stood up and began to exit the room, I noticed that one among the group (whom I will call Chris) had waited for the other students to depart. With a heavy, uneasy posture, Chris approached my desk and asked me if we could speak. I could see how uneasy he seemed, his face sunken and his eyes lifting up toward the ceiling in what it seemed to me was an effort to evade direct eye contact.

"Can I ask you something?"

"Sure," I said, suspecting that Chris was about to share something that would in some ways extend far beyond the content of the classroom, the sonnet, or myself.

"Can you please not talk about death again? I just find it very uncomfortable."

As Chris stood in front of me, both relating to me and trying hard not to at the same time, I took in the gravity of what he was trying to convey. Clearly, something about the sonnet and the discussion regarding it had triggered a visceral response in him. As he stood at my desk, he seemed almost entirely seized by the weight of his feelings—out of my reach, like a distant boat on a rocky sea.

On some fully empathetic level, I wanted to say "Sure. I get it. I will not talk about death anymore in this English class." I wanted to open my arms and give Chris a hug, let him know that whatever the sonnet triggered in him was something temporary that would pass. I wanted Chris to feel okay. But there was another part of me that felt differently, a part that knew that not speaking about death in an English class was impossible, like asking a chemistry teacher not to talk about carbon. I knew we would read many more works of literature in which characters died or talked about death. I also knew that as difficult as death seemed to be for Chris to acknowledge, it would be a word and a concept that would come up in many of the other courses Chris was enrolled in, from history and science to psychology and philosophy. What's more, Chris was susceptible to confronting death on TV shows, in movies, in casual conversations, or during his subway rides to and from school. One day, too, Chris himself would die. As Jim Morrison famously said in 1968, "No one here gets out alive."

Caught between the sincere empathy I had for Chris and a more expansive knowledge of reality, I did what I thought made the most sense in the moment: I listened. I acknowledged how difficult these things can be, and I also allowed the silence and discomfort of the moment to be what it was. I did not offer any false promises to Chris. I did not agree we wouldn't talk anymore about death. And I allowed the exchange to end with a pretty intense sentiment of irresolution because, in some reflective way, I thought that was fairly representative of Chris's current struggle.

Perhaps this will come up again for Chris. Perhaps this was a one-off. Regardless of what it was, it evidenced something important: sometimes the work is painful, and the only thing we can really do is to acknowledge that pain. And maybe that's a part of it, too. Maybe that's the best worst thing we can do as English teachers working with students who have endured traumas.

Revisiting Alison

In the weeks and months following Alison's departure from my classroom, something unexpected happened: we decided to work together. Given our respective histories and the fact that we now shared an important connection in the classroom, Alison and I engaged in a series of interview conversations (Kvale and Brinkman, 2009). We discussed trauma; we shared personal stories about students, and we sought to better understand, prioritize, and plan for scenarios in which student survivors get triggered.

The momentum these conversations engendered paved the way for a paper we collaborated on. The article, "What Happened July 21st—An Investigation of Trigger Warnings and Trauma in the English Classroom," was published in 2019 in *Changing English*. A year later, Alison and I presented the work at the NCTE Convention in Baltimore. Alison has since published two books and is currently the English department chair at a prestigious prep school. We remain friends to this day, touching base regularly and continuing to navigate the complex intersectionality between trauma and the English classroom. What happened on July 21st brought us closer. I believe it's likely that several of these positive consequences may not have occurred had Alison not been triggered. Getting triggered is not necessarily a bad thing.

Trauma is not a black-and-white issue. Neither are trigger warnings. In some ideological sense, the United States is built on the premise that individuals in a society should exercise choice. It is one of the core features that distinguishes American government from dictatorships, monarchies, oligarchies, and authoritarian regimes. Choice and freedom, almost by necessity, encourage difference, differentiation, and divergence of thought and practice.

Put plainly, there is a host of ways English teachers can work with and attend to the reality of student trauma. The trigger warning (whether it is given or not given) represents only one piece of a highly complex and dynamic puzzle. We need to prioritize the puzzle, not the individual pieces. What we are arguing for in this book is that you make a puzzle. How you create that puzzle and which pieces you use should be a matter of individual philosophy and personal choice, like a chef who looks into the refrigerator and selects certain ingredients.

In the pages that follow, Cassie, Kristen, and I will begin to offer more comprehensive ways of looking at, assessing, and enculturing academic spaces conducive to many of the challenges that occur when students with a history of trauma get triggered by engagement with our courses. In chapter 4, Cassie will discuss what might be most important: the centrality of the student-teacher relationship and how relational teaching can build alliances and foster rich, aesthetic engagement for student survivors. In chapter 5, I will examine what we can learn about trauma through the literary characters we read. In chapters 6, 7, and 8, Cassie and Kristen will look at how we navigate and assess student writing, both academic and personal. They will also suggest approaches that are supportive and productive when students share their traumas in their writing. Lastly, in chapters 9 and 10, Kristen will turn the lens inward toward the English teacher, probing important considerations relevant to memory, narrative, and self-care. Should English teachers wish to establish a rigorous and therapeutic learning space for their students, they must also recognize the importance and value of taking care of themselves.

Let's start broadening the conversation. Let's put away the all-or-nothing modes of thought. If the educator sincerely wishes to promote a classroom space that is trauma informed and attuned to the matter of student trauma, let's stop talking about the trigger warning and start talking about everything else.

Chapter 3: Questions for Reflection

1. Why do you think it is so hard to predict what will trigger our students?
2. Why do you think people feel so strongly for or against trigger warnings? Why is the topic so inherently triggering?
3. Think about trauma-informed pedagogy as a complex puzzle. When you think about its complexities, what pieces of the puzzle seem most important to you?
4. If you had been his teacher, what would you have said to Chris when he approached you?
5. When and why might doing "nothing" be preferable to jumping in and trying to do too much to help a student who seems triggered?
6. What did this chapter teach you about trauma-informed pedagogy and practice?

II

Declaration

4

Building Connections through Relational Teaching

From classroom experiences and conversations with students, it is clear that students are more willing to write and share about their traumatic experiences if they feel they have built a trusting relationship with their teacher. In this chapter, Cassandra Lo will review the principles of relational teaching and will focus on how English teachers can use relational gestures to connect with the individuals they teach. These small gestures can impact the classroom climate and students' willingness to participate in assignments, discussions, and activities. Examples of successful and unsuccessful student-teacher relationships will be discussed.

> As a classroom community, our capacity to generate excitement is deeply affected by our interest in one another, in hearing one another's voices, in recognizing one another's presence.
>
> — bell hooks, *Teaching to Transgress*

Peter was a Chinese American student in my eleventh-grade English course during the early days of my teaching career. He was a class clown, always joking around with me and his classmates with a dry, witty sense of humor. He was an excellent artist who drew me a picture of Michael Scott from *The Office* on Teacher Appreciation Day. Instead of his famous "Best Boss Ever" mug, Michael Scott held a "Best Teacher Ever" mug. Peter was captain of the fencing team and spent hours perfecting his craft. Peter also wanted to be an engineer and had a younger sister named Grace who was a freshman at our high school. He would come to see me after school to discuss books he was reading outside of class or for advice on typical high school issues.

Although he repeatedly told me that English was not his favorite subject, Peter was always open to my feedback on his writing and sought out extra help with difficult readings. I felt that I had a pretty good idea of who he was as a person, and I also felt that we had a fairly strong relationship.

After the AP exam, I asked my students to write a draft of their college essay. I gave them the prompts from the Common Application and samples from previous students. The tone of the samples ranged from silly to vulnerable because I wanted to demonstrate that students could write about a variety of topics in multiple ways. Two weeks later, Peter submitted an unexpected essay. He wrote about May, his youngest sister, who was twelve and suffered from a seizure disorder that caused her to be without oral language. Peter explained that his drive and motivation was so he could succeed in ways May would never be able to experience. He wanted to live his life for her:

> There are a lot of things I do not know about this world, like where I fit in and where I'm headed, but I do know there is a reason why my sister is the way she is. It's difficult to describe why because each new day is a learning experience; a journey of self-discovery. In the end, she's here to help me become the person I should be. Though I may not know who that person is, she shows me. She is the consistent white light that shines bright in the dark, myopic tunnel of my life. I work harder and strive for more knowing my every move affects my family and ultimately her life. Life, itself, is like a roller coaster—of which I'm afraid—with its ups and downs. It can be great when I score high on a standardized test or have the confidence to ask a girl out. Or it could be terrible when nothing goes as planned, and I'm just having a bad day. In any case, I know May will always be with me, smiling and constantly reminding me that everything will be okay. She helps me persevere through each and every day.
>
> There is not much to my sister besides her endearing smiles and giddy laughter, but it's that simplicity which has made all the difference. Like a painting, each moment with her tells a different story; a story that, with much reflection, teaches new virtues. I can honestly not ask for more. All I can do is love her and hope that she gets better. I only wish to give to her, in return, all that she has given to me. It is very clichéd to say that one cannot love another more than I love my sister, but as a matter of fact it's true. She defines who I am; what makes me special. No matter where I go or wherever I find myself in the future, I promise to always have her with me.

I was shocked when I read this essay, as Peter had never mentioned May before. I went through an entire school year asking Peter about his sister, thinking there was only one, Grace. I asked Peter if people at school knew about May, and he told me he didn't often talk about her because he was afraid of people making fun of her. We had many discussions about his essay after the initial draft and continued to work on it until he submitted it with his college application the following fall. Peter got into his top-choice school and planned to study engineering.

Two days before his high school graduation, tragedy struck Peter's family. May passed away after experiencing a massive seizure. Peter and his family still attended graduation, but it was painful to watch them try to celebrate an exciting milestone while grieving the tragic loss. A few days after graduation, I attended May's funeral. Her tiny casket was draped in cloth with messages written in Chinese. As I worked my way through the crowds of people paying their respects, I noticed a poster-sized essay next to her casket. Peter's college essay about his sister was on display for all to see. Friends and family members crowded around the poster to read Peter's work and praised him for his beautiful words. His mother embraced me and thanked me for helping him with the essay. She told me she was grateful that he shared his feelings about her before she passed. This incident affirmed for me both the power of relationships within the classroom and the cathartic healing that can take place through personal writing.

The English classroom is a place where trust must be built between students and teachers as they engage in emotion-laden texts and personal writing assignments. When students suspect they are their teacher's priority, it creates comfort and allows for a space where students can engage authentically. Texts and compositions are the mediums through which the work is done, but the relationships are truly the essential part of English classrooms. Teachers can center relationships by employing relational teaching in their classrooms.

The Theory Behind Relational Teaching and Learning

Relational teaching and learning scholars posit that students learn best and teachers teach best when a strong relationship is present between students and teachers. This "working alliance" is at the core of all teaching and learning activities in a school (Rogers, 2009). Engagement and productivity are increased when teachers and students treat each other with respect and understanding (Reichert and Hawley, 2014). Additionally, "[r]esults suggest that perceptions of caring teachers are related to students' academic efforts and to their pursuit of prosocial and social responsibility goals" (Wentzel, 1997, 415). Teachers' presence allows for connections to form within classroom spaces, and focusing on the foundations of every classroom, especially the student-teacher relationships that are present within every environment, is necessary in order to better improve students' schooling experiences (Rogers and Raider-Roth, 2006). Relational teaching not only impacts what goes on within one specific classroom but also influences relationships and goals for students outside of the classroom space. Relational teaching is a pedagogical strategy that should be encouraged in all contexts because it supports community building in the classroom while providing a comfortable space for students to share about issues they are facing.

The need for relational teaching and learning is apparent, and it is especially necessary for students who have experienced trauma. Relational teaching involves acknowledging students' whole lives and creating a climate where students can engage in a comfortable way. Relational learning for underrepresented students, especially boys of color, is critical because, "[w]hile racial marginalization and poverty undeniably bear negatively on scholastic achievement, it is important to note that within each racial and class group, masculine norms compound or 'inflect' these effects—to the extent that boys stand at the very bottom of achievement rankings for all groups of color" (Reichert and Hawley, 2014, 18). Nelson (2016) concludes that the relational teaching at a single-sex middle school for boys of color both established a strong culture for learning and added a counternarrative "which challenged the hypermasculine and nonrelational stereotypes associated with Black males" (27). It is clear that students' emotional wellbeing can be improved through relational teaching.

While relational teaching is effective for all students, Reichert and Hawley (2014) conducted studies that focused on the effect of relational teaching on male students. They gathered evidence of eight relational gestures from an international survey of 1,200 male students in middle or high school and 1,100 teachers. These gestures are:

- Reach out, often improvising measures to meet a particular student's need.
- Demonstrate mastery of their subjects.
- Maintain admirable standards.
- Respond to a student's personal interest or talent.
- Share a common interest with a student.
- Share a common characteristic with a student.
- Accommodate a measure of opposition.
- Reveal a vulnerability.

While many of these gestures seem expected, others focus on aspects of the classroom that wouldn't at first glance appear to contribute to relationships. For example, Reichert and Hawley's survey respondents cited content mastery as a relational gesture because teacher confidence and trustworthiness can be linked to strength in content knowledge. Other gestures, such as when teachers reveal a vulnerability of their own, can directly relate to students who have experienced trauma. This particular gesture humanizes teachers and shows students that they, too, have been through difficult moments. Another successful relational gesture that students have reported is "persistence" in relationships (Gross and Lo, 2018). Students appreciate when teachers check in and reach out frequently, even if the student isn't responsive immediately. This frequency of support allows students to feel comfortable to share when they are ready but are not required to share just because the teacher is inquiring once.

Teachers, too, benefit from relational pedagogy, especially when working with students who have experienced loss. Teachers who have strong relationships with their students can translate these relationships into academic success because they demonstrate clear expectations and support (Gross and Lo, 2018). While it can be a successful technique in a classroom, teacher preparation programs rarely address "how to recognize and address trauma in classrooms," even though teachers must face grief head on in the workplace (LaMay, 2016, 68). When teachers assume a relational stance in their classrooms, the power dynamic shifts away from an aggressive, authoritative focus of traditional teaching to a more collaborative and open one (Smagorinsky, 2019). Relational learning and teaching can significantly improve school experiences for students who have experienced loss, and it is especially beneficial for those who are often overlooked or over-disciplined in schools.

Successful and Unsuccessful Relational Experiences—Teacher A versus Teacher B

"I'm going to call your mom and dad," Teacher A's voice echoed through the room as the students completed their classwork. Andrew was not working as diligently as the teacher had hoped, and Teacher A threatened to report home about his lack of productivity. Andrew laughed and replied, "good luck." He received a Saturday detention for that interaction.

What Teacher A did not know, or did not take into consideration in that moment, was that Andrew was living alone at age eighteen. His mother passed away from cancer when he was sixteen, and his father was not a part of his life. He was originally under the care of his aunt and uncle, who were often absent, until he turned 18. Now, Andrew was taking care of himself and the house his mother left him, on top of completing his high school assignments. Instead of asking Andrew why he wasn't working in the manner that was expected of him or asking why Andrew uttered "good luck" in response to Teacher A's threat, he was issued a detention and asked to sit in silence as a punishment.

It is common for teachers to say they are going to call home when a student is acting in a way that they don't approve of or does not complete their assigned work. Unfortunately for students who have experienced trauma, the threat of calling home comes with reminders of grief and loss. In one school where I did research, I asked students who had lost a family member if it was important for their teachers to know about their traumas. Both Andrew and another student discussed the teacher at their school who always threatened to call "mom and dad" if a student was misbehaving. This statement is problematic for many reasons. A student could be living with one parent, with two parents of the same sex, with an extended family member, in foster care, or they could have lost a parent. This statement, meant to punish students, does more than just punish them in the classroom. It leaves a lasting impression on students.

Conversely, Andrew had a very successful relationship with Teacher B, another teacher at school who demonstrated empathy for his students. Teacher B and Andrew were from different cultural backgrounds, as Andrew identifies as Black and the teacher identifies as White, but Andrew admired his teacher for being culturally responsive. Andrew and Teacher B also shared a male identity, and Andrew mentioned that Teacher B acted as a father figure by giving him life advice and supporting him in his activities. Teacher B took student input into consideration when it came to decorating his classroom and playing music during work time. The students felt comfortable showing up to class and sticking around afterward. Reichert and Hawley (2013) find that those in-between and after-class moments are particularly important, because "teachers tend to succeed relationally with boys when they come to know them beyond their scholastic performance and classroom behavior" (62).

Teacher B stood in the hallway between classes and exchanged handshakes and high fives with the students as they walked by. The relationship between Andrew and Teacher B grew because he was allowed to spend his free time in the classroom, and this teacher also served as a support system when Andrew lost his mother. As his mother's health worsened, and she had to go back to the hospital, Teacher B joined him in the waiting room. Several teachers attended the funeral and helped Andrew as he started living on his own. They purchased gift cards to local grocery stores and places to purchase school supplies. At that point in his life, the adults Andrew relied upon were all school personnel. These teachers and school staff members demonstrated the use of relational gestures by reaching out to Andrew and meeting his needs where they were in order to support him.

Andrew's gratitude for the school staff was particularly apparent during his high school graduation ceremony. His school gives each student flowers to share with loved ones who helped them succeed. As his classmates walked into the audience and received hugs from their family members, Andrew made his way over to the teacher section of the audience and gave his flowers to faculty members.

Andrew's experiences with teachers are not unique. Stories that students have shared with me over the past decade have exposed the joys and challenges of student-teacher relationships. Positive relationships have grown from participating in extracurricular activities together, from teachers attending student events such as plays and athletic competitions, and from teachers leaving their doors open during lunch and after school. While showing up for students outside of class time is valuable, it is not something that can be expected from all teachers, nor is it the only way that relationships can form. Teachers who hold admirable standards and share about connecting vulnerabilities have proven to be equally successful as those who form bonds outside of the classroom.

Unfortunately, while so many students recall positive relationships with teachers, many also have challenging relationships to share as well. Relationships that are less successful often stem from a lack of trust between student and teacher. For students who have experienced trauma, losing the trust of a teacher can be even more difficult. One student recalled that a teacher whom they trusted and respected shared about the unfortunate murder of the student's father in front of classmates, who were unknowledgeable about the situation. The student reported that they felt betrayed and stopped participating in class. Another student shared that their teacher did not believe they were suffering from a chronic illness because they couldn't see it. Despite a doctor's note, this teacher was not accommodating or supportive, even as the student fell so ill they had to cease attending school and had to participate in home instruction. The students who shared these stories with me held onto these experiences for years and cited that they led to a general hesitancy around all teachers.

These examples highlight the importance of teachers providing space for their students to share about their losses, traumas and lived experiences. Moments of retraumatization can be reduced if teachers are mindful of their phrasings and comments to students. Unsuccessful relationships can lead to students' negative feelings about school in general. In contrast, relationships can strengthen academic success and can improve school experiences for students who have experienced trauma. Based on the stories that students shared, it is clear that relational teaching is a pedagogy that supports students and is helpful in establishing a strong classroom environment.

Relational Teaching in the English Classroom

While building relationships are encouraged for all teachers, it is especially important in the English classroom. Reading texts and interacting with certain characters within texts can resurface difficult memories for students. Writing compositions, especially personal narratives, can elicit similar feelings for students. This idea will be expanded upon in later chapters as we discuss writing activities, assignments, and rubrics that can support students who have experienced trauma. Relational teaching can strengthen the unique community needs within an English classroom space and can allow for trust between students and teachers when engaging in difficult readings or writing assignments.

When a teacher confidently executes their plans and expertly analyzes texts with students, it is admirable. Mastery of content material can increase student trust and confidence in teachers (Reichert and Hawley, 2013). Students can let their guards down a bit when in the presence of a teacher who demonstrates mastery of their English content. Students are more likely to engage in classroom activities and discussions when a teacher shares a well-planned lesson. Writing assignments with clear directions and assessment criteria serve as a space for students to share while knowing the parameters and expectations from their teacher.

Relationships can also be forged through accommodating a measure of opposition (Reichert and Hawley, 2013). As students engage in a variety of texts, they will often share mixed responses. Some students love texts while others despise them. Some students feel sympathy for Holden Caulfield in *Catcher in the Rye* while others find him aggravating. Some understand the secrets Clare Kendry keeps in *Passing* while others believe she should live her truth. Rich conversations can occur when students question information presented to them. Teachers are encouraged to allow student opposition to texts if it promotes productive discussion. When implemented effectively, a Socratic seminar can be a beautiful place for students to express their true feelings about texts without the traditional back-and-forth of student-teacher discussions. By accepting (a bit of) opposition from students and engaging their thoughts on topics, no matter how disparate they may be, teachers demonstrate genuine care for their students.

Revealing a vulnerability can be scary for teachers at first but can also be an integral part of creating strong relationships with students. If students know that teachers have experienced loss or have other difficulties, it shows students they are not alone in their challenges. Dutro (2008) writes how she shared about the loss of her brother in a literature circle with students who were discussing their own losses. The conversation was provoked by the reading of a text in which a character was an orphan. Reciprocity in sharing vulnerabilities between teachers and students can be an important practice in a literacy classroom (Dutro, 2019). Revealing a vulnerability is best done when students are doing the same because it balances the power dynamic between student and teacher. Dutro (2019) asks, "While the consequences of my vulnerability in the classroom are not comparable to the students', how can I ask children to take those risks if I'm not willing to?" (9). Modeling is such a common practice in classrooms, and sharing a vulnerability with students is a great example of effective modeling. When sharing, however, it is important to be mindful of what is shared and when so as not to burden students with additional traumas.

Exercises to Foster Classroom Relationships

Getting-to-know-you surveys

Introductory surveys are a great way for teachers to get to know their students and learn about their preferences. These surveys can be administered on paper or on an internet form, but they should be done individually so that students can share as freely as possible without fear of critique from their peers. Basic questions such as pronouns and chosen names/nicknames can ensure that students feel comfortable when called on in class. Deeper questions can reveal challenges that students face in their learning. Introductory surveys tell students that teachers care about their whole selves beyond the class time they spend together each day. The questions below, some of which are found in Smagorinsky's *Teaching English by Design* (2019), are examples of effective getting-to-know-you survey questions:

- What do you enjoy doing outside of class?
- What expectations do you have for yourself in and out of school?
- What is your greatest quality?
- Complete this statement: "I am an expert on . . ."
- What is one thing people don't know about you?
- As your teacher, how can I support your learning in this classroom? What do you need from me to be successful?
- Is there anything else you'd like to share with me?

Asking these questions allows students to share about themselves and their strengths while also providing insight to teachers about their students' lives. The last question, "Is there anything else you'd like to share with me?" is the most important one. Giving students the option to share whatever is on their mind is necessary for some students, especially those who have experienced trauma and want to divulge that information to their teacher in a private space.

Integrating personal interests and needs into the curriculum

In addition to gathering critical information about students, interest inventories like the ones mentioned above can help teachers "generate essential questions in light on kids' perspectives and choose relevant authors and texts that match their interests and needs" (Smagorinsky, 2019, 233). For English classes, this information can be used to make curricular decisions that will engage students and that can be mindful of traumas students may have experienced. For example, if students share that their families emigrated to the US, then incorporating essays and stories about the immigrant experience can be relatable. If students share that they are artists and enjoy comic books, teachers can consider including graphic novels and comics in your curriculum.

Optional sharing

When asking students to write personal responses or to share personal experiences, optional sharing is a way to minimize stressful interactions around compositions. Sharing is an important part of the writing process, as students can see that their writing is valuable and important to more than just the teacher. Optional sharing allows for those who feel compelled to share to have a platform for their testimonials. At the same time, it allows for the writing exercise itself to serve as a potentially cathartic experience that students do not have to worry about divulging to their classmates if they are not prepared to do so. If for some reason sharing is absolutely necessary for a specific assignment, then it must be explicitly clear to students that they will be asked to share before writing.

Writing conferences

Writing conferences are commonplace in elementary classrooms, but they aren't seen as frequently in secondary spaces. Writing conferences can allow for students to share verbally about their writing and work through any challenges they may be having. Some students find it easier to talk through their struggles rather than to write about it, so these conversations can be powerful places for writing development. Writing conferences can take place while the rest of the class engages in group work, independent reading, or research.

Shared documents for editing conversations

Digital platforms are frequently used in English classrooms today, and many of those platforms have cloud-based document options. When students craft narratives as shareable documents, they can communicate with their teachers through comments and chats as they write. This is a more private way for students to communicate any challenges they have while writing and for teachers to share more personalized feedback at the draft level. This practice is recommended for engaging with students who are less comfortable sharing aloud in the classroom.

Establishing a Caring Classroom Community

I placed index cards with each student's name on the front at their seats to greet them on the first day of school each year. I asked students to complete their introductory surveys on the back of that card so I could easily refer to their information when needed. When the final bell rang on that first day of school, I would pick up my set of index cards and learn about my new students. The composition of each class was always so drastically different, and these surveys helped me to determine how I would approach each one. Above all, these surveys were a window into a set of students who I did not yet know. It was the groundwork for the possibilities of what was to come. I still maintain this practice as a college professor and have similar results from my high school days. For some students, this is simply an activity that is completed because they were instructed to do so. For others, especially those who may feel particularly uneasy about the transition back from the summer or who may be experiencing grief or PTSD, this exercise allowed the sharing of stories that were necessary for my understanding of their lived experiences.

As established in this chapter (and throughout the book as a whole), student-teacher relationships are critical to the success of an English classroom. As the school year begins, some students hesitantly enter classrooms as they greet new teachers. They don't know if the teachers are trustworthy or if they will take the time to get to know the class. For students who have experienced trauma, this sense of trust is particularly important, as they may feel compelled to reveal deeply personal stories about themselves. Through gestures and relationships, teachers can work to build trust and comfort from the very first day, which will lead to students feeling that they can present their authentic selves when responding to literature or crafting compositions.

Cridland-Hughes (2015) defines a caring, critical literacy in ELA classroom as "using the collective voice and the collective vision of a community to align goals, to support each other, and to teach love" (131–132). Of course, "teaching love" is not necessarily a part of the curricula that teachers are expected to implement, but it is the best way to show our students that they matter and that their stories matter. I often wonder what would have happened if Andrew's teacher had been more careful about comments relating to family members in their classroom. Similarly, I wonder what could have happened if I had known about Peter's sister May before the end of the school year. Both Peter and Andrew were silenced in their grief and struggles because their teachers were unaware of their needs. In chapter 6, we will consider how these relationships can contribute to positive writing experiences for students. Relational teaching is a critical component of both reading and writing activities in English classrooms, as it builds trust and strengthens the classroom community. This classroom community that forms through the use of relational teaching allows for the sort of vulnerability and reciprocal exchanging of ideas that are critical to supporting students who have experienced trauma.

Chapter 4: Questions for Reflection

1. Have you witnessed positive or negative relational interactions between students and teachers in the past? Could those moments have been approached differently by the teacher?
2. What goals do you have for yourself when it comes to establishing a strong classroom community?
3. Which activities from the "exercises that foster classroom relationships" section can you implement into your classroom? What, if any, difficulties can you anticipate when implementing these activities?

5

Learning about Trauma through the Characters We Read

Trauma is everywhere: in the news, on TV, in our personal lives, and in our classrooms. It is also in the books we read and the texts we teach. Although we do not always recognize them as such, many of the books, short stories, poems, and plays we share with our students are packed with traumatic experiences that have challenged the lives of protagonists from Sethe and Celie to Edgar and Willy Loman. In fact, given the exceptional skill with which authors utilize words to capture human emotion, thought, and experience, some of the most illustrative portrayals of trauma take place in the books we read and teach. In our ever-burgeoning effort to expand our understanding of trauma, its weight, impact, and contours, I (Adam Wolfsdorf) will use chapter 5 to explore how we can learn more about trauma through many of the books we cherish and share with our students.

> (T)he purpose of playing, whose end, both at the first and now, was and is, to hold as 'twere the mirror up to nature: to show virtue her feature, scorn her own image, and the very age and body of the time his form and pressure.
>
> —William Shakespeare, *Hamlet*

Though we might not realize it, much of the time that we are teaching literature, we hold trauma in our hands. From Sethe (*Beloved*) and Amir (*The Kite Runner*) to Cordelia (*King Lear*), Hester Prynne (*The Scarlet Letter*), Blanche (*A Streetcar Named Desire*), Willy Loman (*Death of a Salesman*), Janie (*Their Eyes Were Watching God*), and Celie (*The Color Purple*), English teachers—whether we intend to or not—read, share, and talk about traumatized individuals every day. If the characters are like Hamlet, Nick (*The Great Gatsby*), Paul (*All Quiet on the Western Front*), or Alison (*Fun Home*), they are acutely aware they are living through or recounting traumatic circumstances that have upended their lives and forced them to reckon with the dark side of a cruel world. The purpose of their literary journeys, in some seminal way, is to use words to make sense of the unspeakable. Gatsby floating dead at the top of his pool. Starr looking down at the lifeless body of Khalil. Amir staring into the abandoned alley. The unspeakable spoken.

Other characters may be less aware of their traumas—they may, in fact, cause them. Rather than having the capacity to pull back from the atrocities and gain some narrative distance, characters such as Blanche, Willy Loman, and Holden Caulfield seem to endure traumas without the benefit of mindfulness. They suffer in ways that are reactive, disenfranchised, and even oblivious to the forces operating in and around them. For every scene in which Willy castigates his sons, babbles about being well liked, or pontificates about some imagined glory or demise, he literally and figuratively sits behind the wheel of a car he cannot operate. If protagonists such as Tara Westover or Alison Bechdel gain insight and evolve as a result of their traumatic family lives, Willy is seized by his troubles, incapable of grasping, utilizing, or gaining wisdoms from his personal storm. Either way, the teacher who teaches these books and the students who read them can learn a lot about trauma along the way.

It is curious to consider why we, as English teachers, sometimes fail to recognize the central role that trauma plays in so many of the books we teach. When working with graduate students at NYU, I have often asked them to pause and consider whether they can come up with a single literary text that does not dive viscerally into trauma. I watch as they deliberate the question; for many, it is the first time they've considered it. Invariably, most come to the same conclusion: literature and trauma are often intrinsically wed. And yet why don't we automatically know that?

Maybe the failure to see what is right in front of us results from the immaculate beauty of the writer's craft? Perhaps the story is simply so compelling that we are hypnotically drawn in? Like so many of the most beautiful, heartfelt, and intoxicating songs, expertly crafted narratives often lull us into a meditative union, one in which we lose track of just how brutal, raw, and destabilizing the circumstances of the drama may be. Or perhaps our inability to recognize trauma in literature relates to the fact that many people are, in some ways, blind or even ignorant to their own traumatic experiences. The blind reader blindly reads what the characters cannot see. Or perhaps we don't have a clear handle on what trauma is in the first place, so we fail to identify it properly when it occurs in fiction. A cognitive psychologist might say that when we read fiction, we are often engaged in a right brain activity, pulled in close to the narrative and therefore temporarily disengaged from the left brain analytic process that typically allows for narrative distance and recognition of trauma.

In chapter 5, I will utilize a handful of literary characters in order to demonstrate some core features of trauma: how it *arrests us in its grip*, the way it compels us to seek control, its capacity for *causing numb or dissociative responses*, and the extent to which it can cause us to become *hyper-aroused* or to *shut us down*. Each of these states and the complexities that attend to them foster feelings of isolation, loneliness, turbulence, and despair. Through focusing on a selection of prominent literary characters, I will illustrate how the books we teach and the words we read can serve as glasses wherein we may hold the mirror up to trauma, and, in the process, more deeply understand both our students and ourselves.

FROZEN IN TRAUMA: *THE KITE RUNNER* AND *A STREETCAR NAMED DESIRE*

Being frozen in time is a fundamental response to trauma. Since trauma can feel so overwhelming and all-consuming, trauma survivors often become psychologically arrested in response to traumatic circumstances. Like an animal that freezes in the face of danger, traumatized individuals can shut down completely and become psychologically arrested. We see evidence of this type of psychological response in many texts. From Septimus (Mrs. Dalloway) and Marlow (*Heart of Darkness*) to Ophelia (*Hamlet*), the Swede (*American Pastoral*), and Starr (*The Hate U Give*), scores of literary characters endure circumstances that upend their lives and shock them into psychological arrest. Life progresses, but the survivor is incapable of moving forward.

Observe the opening lines of Khaled Hosseini's novel *The Kite Runner*:

> I became what I am today at the age of twelve, on a frigid overcast day in the winter of 1975. I remember the precise moment, crouching behind a crumbling mud wall, peeking into the alley near the frozen creek. That was a long time ago, but it's wrong what they say about the past, I've learned, about how you can bury it. Because the past claws its way out. Looking back now, I realize I have been peeking into that deserted alley for the last twenty-six years. (1)

Like Marsha from chapter 2, whose PET scan revealed that her brain remained frozen in time on the day thirteen years prior when her daughters were killed in a car crash, Amir cannot free himself from the rape he witnesses. What he sees in that dark alley—the brutal beating and sexual assault of his childhood friend and kite-running partner, Hassan—takes hold of Amir's reality and forever shifts the course and focus of his world. For students in our classes who have been victims of sexual abuse, domestic violence, racial persecution, or other visceral episodes of impact trauma, life can be turned upside down. Trust can be lost, and the survivor may struggle to retain a sense of safety and progress. The powerful play goes on, but the actor stands alone on the stage, forgetful of their lines and incapable of moving forward.

We see a similar phenomenon in Tennessee Williams' portrayal of Blanche in *A Streetcar Named Desire.* For Blanche, who shows up unexpectedly at Stanley and Stella's home in New Orleans, her emotional paralysis begins on the day her husband shoots himself:

> We danced the Varsouviana! Suddenly in the middle of the dance the boy I had married broke away from me and ran out of the casino. A few moments later—a shot! [Blanche rises stiffly. Then, the polka resumes in a major key.] I ran out—all did!—all ran and gathered about the terrible thing at the edge of the lake! . . . He'd stuck the revolver into his mouth, and fired—so that the back of his head had been—blown away! . . . And then the searchlight which had been turned on the world was turned off again and never for one moment since has there been any light that's stronger than this—kitchen candle . . . (115)

Throughout the course of the play, Blanche's traumatic episodes pull her out of the present tense, robbing her of agency and destabilizing her. No matter where she goes—Belle Reve, Laurel, New Orleans—the past accompanies her, traumatic memories penetrate her mind in the form of hallucinations, flashbacks, and traumatic relivings. In a way that is typical for many trauma survivors, the past becomes indistinguishable from the present. It interferes with her emotional and sexual development, costing her her career, alienating her from family, friends, and loved ones, and making it impossible to establish intimacy with a romantic partner. Gripped by her past, Blanche spends much of Streetcar abusing alcohol, "soaking in a hot tub" (29), and indulging her inappropriate sexual urges for adolescent boys. As van der Kolk writes in *The Body Keeps the Score*:

> Traumatized people chronically feel unsafe inside their bodies: The past is alive in the form of gnawing interior discomfort. Their bodies are constantly bombarded by visceral warning signs, and, in an attempt to control these processes, they often become expert at ignoring their gut feelings and in numbing awareness of what is played out inside. They learn to hide from their selves. (p.97)

A Need for Possession: Control and Psychological Abuse in *Hamlet*

Because trauma can be so overwhelming and disorienting, trauma survivors often seek control (Herman, 1992; Levine, 2010; van der Kolk, 2014). Many of the literary characters we read do as well. Despite his extraordinary intelligence and remarkable wit (Bloom, 2003; Lewis, 1976), Hamlet feels deeply out of control for much of Shakespeare's play. To overcompensate for his spiraling psychological feelings, Hamlet becomes obsessed with mastering a world that is quickly spinning away from his grasp. The play contains 4,042 lines, of which Hamlet speaks some 1,480. From his "too, too sullied flesh" (1.2.129), to his "form and movement" (2.2.327), Hamlet uses language in a desperate attempt to stabilize his world.

At various junctures of the play, his principal target is Ophelia. When relating to her, he uses crafty, convoluted language to dominate her, sending mixed, confusing messages that disorient her. In the nunnery scene, Hamlet toys with Ophelia's mind. He simultaneously pulls her in and pushes her away:

HAMLET
The fair Ophelia! Nymph, in thy orisons
Be all my sins remember'd . . .

OPHELIA
My lord, I have remembrances of yours,
That I have longed long to re-deliver;
I pray you, now receive them.

HAMLET
No, not I;
I never gave you aught. (3.1.96–105)

Something about this interaction smacks of the type of unstable, adolescent romance we at times observe among our students. The language is tinged with both sexual innuendo and aggression. In the same sentence, he refers to her as "fair" or virginal, only to recast her as a sexually promiscuous "nymph." He offers her his prayers ("orisons") but then quickly implores her to remember his "sins." This duality of speech and language suggests the type of cognitive dissonance and confusion that trauma survivors experience when they have been wounded by the people in their lives who are supposed to love them most (Herman, 1992; Levine, 2010). In some ways, Ophelia is merely a pawn in a much more complex game in which Gertrude, the queen, roams the chess board of Hamlet's mind and wreaks havoc on his faith, emotional solidity, and capacity for trusting and living cohesively within the world (Wolfsdorf, 2018). In this sense, Hamlet's inability to trust Ophelia seems like a transferential offshoot of his radical mistrust of his mother. Like the classic adolescent who has been mistreated by his parents, Hamlet fears that Ophelia will hurt him the way Gertrude has. Hypervigilant and self-protective, Hamlet studies Ophelia closely for any signs of betrayal. He loves her and is drawn in by her, but he is simultaneously terrified by the idea of closeness and fights against intimacy. He epitomizes the concept of ambivalence.

In *Trauma and Recovery*, Judith Herman recognizes the centrality of ambivalence in traumatic response: "the conflict between the will to deny horrible events and the will to proclaim them aloud is the central dialectic of psychological trauma" (1). Ambivalence leads to aggression, and Hamlet toys with Ophelia's mind, confessing "I did love you once" (3.1.125), only to retract it with "I loved you not" (3.1.129). In staged productions of this scene, Hamlet waffles between affectionate tenderness (gazing, embracing, kissing) and violent, abusive actions. In Kenneth Branagh's 1996 film production, the prince grabs Ophelia by the hair and drags her across the palace floor. He calls her a puppet—"you jig, you amble, and you lisp, and nick-name God's creatures, and make your wantonness your ignorance" (3.1.155); he also sentences her to a "nunnery" (3.1.131). Depending on the interpretation, the nunnery is either a convent or a brothel, another exemplification of Hamlet's ambivalence.

In his cascading relationship with Ophelia, Hamlet is both love and hate, sex and aggression, intimacy and distance. He draws her in, only to push her away. He seeks confidence in her, only to alienate her. This dualistic behavior is remarkably controlling and disorienting. It serves as a quintessential literary example of how a traumatized individual can become abusive and overbearing as a way of coping with their own traumatic experience. Ophelia becomes the puppet to Hamlet's frustrations—the more powerless, vulnerable, and tormented he feels, the more he unconsciously takes possession of Ophelia and drives her into madness.

The irony of Hamlet's mistreatment of Ophelia is that he may, in fact, love her most. It is something curious to consider why the individual who suffers immense pain might turn his aggression toward the person in his life whom he adores most dearly. There is something to consider here about the mechanism of trauma and why people who love each other tend to hurt each other, too.

Dissociation: The Mind of a Salesman

When traumatized individuals confront threats that appear too daunting for them to handle, they psychologically detach from the present and shield themselves from reality. Judith Herman writes: "The ORDINARY RESPONSE TO ATROCITIES is to banish them from consciousness. Certain violations of the social compact are too terrible to utter aloud: this is the meaning of the word unspeakable" (1). In her book *Repressed Memories: A Journey to Recovery from Sexual Abuse*, Renee Frederickson writes: "Dissociation gets you through a brutal experience, letting your basic survival skills operate unimpeded. . . . Your ability to survive is enhanced as the ability to feel is diminished . . . All feelings are blocked; you 'go away.' You are disconnected from the act, the perpetrator & yourself" (59). Elizabeth Howell goes so far as to claim:

> Dissociation, in a general sense, refers to a rigid separation of parts of experiences, including somatic experiences, consciousness, affects, perception, identity, and memory. When there is a structural dissociation, each of the dissociated self-states has at least a rudimentary sense of "I" (Van der Hart et al., 2004). In my view, all of the environmentally based "psychopathology" or problems in living can be seen through this lens. (ix)

Sigmund Freud had a term for this type of dissociation. In his 1900 book *Interpretation of Dreams*, Freud referred to it as "regression in service of the ego," a classic defense mechanism whereby an overwhelmed part of the psyche experiences a temporary or long-term reversion of the ego to an earlier stage of development. The regression is an attempt by the psyche to shield itself from an overwhelming reality and to handle unacceptable impulses more adaptively.

In Arthur Miller's *Death of a Salesman*, we see evidence of just this type of dissociation. In some ways, Willy Loman is the classic 1940s American salesman: visionary, industrious, eager to please, bought into the potentialities within the American ideal. Yet as Willy's attainment of the American dream slips progressively further from his grasp and as issues in his home life deteriorate, Willy struggles to maintain a cohesive sense of self. An analysis of Willy's dissociative tendencies provides a rich illustration of the dissociative traumatic response.

At the top of his play, Arthur Miller explains that:

> The entire setting is wholly or, in some places, partially transparent. . . . Whenever the action is in the present the actors observe the imaginary wall-lines, entering the house only through its door at the left. But in the scenes of the past these boundaries are broken, and characters enter or leave a room by stepping "through" a wall onto the forestage. (1)

Miller chooses to utilize the stage setting as a symbol for Willy's mental reality. The opening stage directions serve metaphorically to capture and encapsulate the vulnerability and fragility of Loman's mind, which is "partially transparent," "imaginary," and "broken."

As an individual who has endured multiple traumas—from his father's abandonment to his failed career trajectory and the affair he has with a woman in Boston—Willy perseveres through a complicated pattern of self-deception and detachment from reality. These patterns are particularly pronounced whenever Willy confronts troubling circumstances that stand in conflict with the heightened magnitude of his idealized self. The first such instance occurs in the play's opening scene, after Willy returns from a failed road trip to Boston. It is late at night, and Willy sits in the kitchen, despondent, unraveled, and defeated. Miller writes:

Willy's form is dimly seen below in the darkened kitchen. . . .

Willy: Just wanna be careful with those girls, Biff, that's all. Don't make any promises. No promises of any kind. Because a girl, y'know, they always believe what you tell 'em, and you're very young, Biff, you're too young to be talking seriously to girls.

[Light rises on the kitchen. Willy, talking, shuts the refrigerator door and comes downstage to the kitchen table. He pours milk into a glass. He is totally immersed in himself, smiling faintly.] (15–16)

As the play unfolds, the target of Willy's incomplete and fragmented identity centralizes around Biff, the vagrant son who at one point embodied all the possibilities and potentialities contained within Willy's most exotic dreams. Like Willy, Biff is ticketed for a life of unrealized potential and failed possibilities. But unlike his father, Biff is capable of staring down reality and acknowledging his defeats and shortcomings:

> **WILLY** [with hatred, threateningly]: The door of your life is wide open!
>
> **BIFF:** Pop! I'm a dime a dozen, and so are you!
>
> **WILLY** [turning on him now in an uncontrolled outburst]: I am not a dime a dozen! I am Willy Loman, and you are Biff Loman! . . .
>
> **BIFF:** I am not a leader of men, Willy, and neither are you. You were never anything but a hard-working drummer who landed in the ash can like all the rest of them! I'm one dollar an hour, Willy! . . .
>
> **BIFF** [at the peak of his fury]: Pop, I'm nothing! I'm nothing, Pop. Can't you understand that? There's no spite in it any more. I'm just what I am, that's all. (105)

This divergence between father and son– the former incapable of accepting reality and the latter insistent on doing so– exemplifies a fundamental split: the traumatized individual cannot tolerate reality, while the healthy psychological mind seeks it out.

In his developmental stage theory, the social psychologist Erik Erikson described the eighth and final stage of life through the lens of *integrity versus despair.* If, for a myriad range of potential reasons, the individual is incapable of doing so, they experience the final stage of life shackled by shame, regret, and despair. Erikson writes: "He who is ashamed would like to force the world not to look at him, not to notice his exposure. He would like to destroy the eyes of the world" (227). This sense of shame, despair, and regret is central to Willy's psychological crisis throughout the play. As the weight of it bears down on him, he retreats from it and dissociates further. He journeys back to when his children were younger—"remember those two beautiful elm trees . . . " (Miller, 6); he rhapsodizes over Biff's Simonizing job on the Chevy and on Biff's heroic Ebbets Field game. Invariably these dissociations, which start out positive and idyllic, crack under the burden of his need for them, and almost as rapidly as the dissociations emerge, they transform into painful, tormenting reminders of ways in which he has not risen to the promises of his unquiet mind. Ultimately, the salesman's dreams dissemble, and he's left with despair, regret, and shattered remnants of a broken life.

A Tale of Two Responses: Hyperarousal or Catatonia

In the summer of 2016, I had the opportunity to interview Bessel van der Kolk. At the time, I was deep into my dissertation research, analyzing the efficacy of trigger warnings in the English classroom. Since I had read many of his works and had been deeply influenced by his thinking, I was curious to hear what van der Kolk thought about trigger warnings. As we began to probe the matter, we got to talking about trauma. It was during this conversation that van der Kolk said something I will never forget: when I asked how we might recognize trauma within a student population, he said, "You see it in dogs during thunderstorms" (van der Kolk, personal communication, August 12, 2015). I was floored by the simple precision of this statement. Like the dog that finds itself caught in a wild storm, trauma survivors either shut down (whimpering and shivering in the rain) or hyperactivate (yelping, barking, and raging against the storm).

From my personal experience in the classroom, I think it is more common for students to shut down than to become hyper-aroused. Although we may not know for sure if students are exhibiting signs of trauma, I can recall many instances where students became unusually quiet, had difficulty focusing, shut down, or withdrew. Elizabeth Dutro has written extensively on the importance of connection in the English classroom (2019). As English teachers, we seek to foster environments where students excitedly commune with the work, but trauma-informed pedagogy understands that sometimes our students will need to dissociate—not as an act of hostility or rejection but because engaging feels too overwhelming or intense.

These same classical responses to trauma—shutting down or hyperactivating—can be observed in many of the texts we teach. The fight-or-flight, sympathetic response is something we see in King Lear, when the king is banished by his daughters and rages against the pitiless storm:

> Blow, winds, and crack your cheeks! rage! blow!
> You cataracts and hurricanoes, spout
> Till you have drench'd our steeples, drown'd the cocks!
> You sulphurous and thought-executing fires. . . .
> That make ingrateful man! (*Lear,* 3.2.1–9)

This is the dog caught in the thunderstorm, raging against the universe and striking out against the lightning and rain. If we had electrodes connected to Lear's brain and body, we'd see that his heart rate and blood pressure elevate, his respiration rate heightens. We'd observe increased sweat gland production and elevated cortisol levels. His brain would be hyper-oxygenated in multiple regions, firing wildly.

If we put Starr into a PET scan machine following the murder of Khalil, she would likely stare absently into the abyss. Her brain might produce a blank, deactivated, and depersonalized response. Her respiration rate might decelerate; her pulse rate might decrease. We might see the same in Hester Prynne as she stands upon the scaffold, in Amir as he looks into that dark alleyway in Kabul, or in Offred as she lies in bed being penetrated by Commander Fred Waterford. Sometimes numbing, dissociating, and depersonalizing are the most adaptive choices for the survivor. Observe Offred's depersonalization in the following sequence:

> I used to think of my body as an instrument, of pleasure, or a means of transportation, or an implement for the accomplishment of my will. . . . Now the flesh arranges itself differently. I'm a cloud, congealed around a central object, the shape of a pear, which is hard and more real than I am and glows red within its translucent wrapping. (Atwood et al., 1992, 88)

Her body is not hers; her choices and decisions are not within her control. In the way that traumatized individuals can feel like they are having an out-of-body experience, Offred distances herself from her pain and detaches.

What Can Literature Teach Us about the Students in the Room?

I am not trying to overstate the connection. Like you, I am aware that the characters in the books we read are not the same as the students who populate our classrooms. When we speak to Hester Prynne, we know she will not answer. When we read King Lear's monologues, he does not suddenly use new words—he follows the same narrative journey every time. Literary characters live in books, not in the world we inhabit. They don't know anything about our lives; they haven't sat in our classrooms; they don't know what we look like. They aren't trying to get good grades, date the person sitting next to them, or make the varsity basketball team. When we leave the classroom and head home, they stay right there on the bookshelf. And though we may change year after year, they are indelibly captured in words.

That said, the characters we read about and the traumatic circumstances they endure can help us to better understand the world around us. And since these characters often endure immense hardships, they can teach us a great deal about the student survivors who populate our classrooms. Whether it's Esther Greenwood and Sethe or Ahab, Molly Bloom, Pip, and Sonny, communing with characters in literature can help us to become more sensitive, more attuned, and more alive and aware in the face of real traumas (Felman and Laub, 1991; Dutro, 2008). We may not always know what to do or how to do it, but learning about trauma through the characters we read might compel us to ask and entertain important questions. If we recognize the dog in the thunderstorm, we can decide whether it is best to approach, give space, speak, or say nothing. Recognition might help us to determine when a student needs support? Might help us to intuit when it's beneficial for them to hang in and tough it out? Might lead us to ask if they want to express what they're feeling? Or stay quiet? There is never one answer or one solution. But gaining some ability to observe and recognize a traumatic response allows us to be more flexible and attuned, putting us in a position to offer students opportunities to build more resilience and know that we care. And if we care, we will do our best, even if doing our best is only partially or marginally helpful.

When we take the time and make the effort to understand student trauma, we engage in action that van der Kolk refers to as "trauma conscious" (291). Trauma consciousness, when attempted, can lead us to a higher level of empathy, respect, attunement, and collaboration. No ideal solutions. No perfectly tied ribbons. No guarantees. No promises. But instead a sincere effort, an honorable mission. In the highly complex and destabilizing world of traumatic response, trying can be an act of grace. And if the books we read can lead us closer to the student survivors we encounter, then that is a win of sorts—a discovery and a first step, one page at a time.

Chapter 5: Questions for Reflection

1. Think about some of the novels, plays, short stories, and poems that you teach. Which characters seem to be traumatized? What are their circumstances, and what behaviors/symptoms do they exhibit? What can you learn about trauma through reading about these characters?
2. When students in your class read books featuring literary characters who endure similar traumas to what your students face in real life, what impact do you think it has on your students? Is it positive, negative, or both?
3. In 1916, Samuel Crothers proposed the concept of bibliotherapy, an adjunctive form of therapy wherein a therapist might prescribe a patient to read a book in order to process and recover from a potential trauma. Do you think this would work? Why or why not?
4. Do you think that reading about traumatized characters impacts the way that trauma survivors write? If so, how?

6

Trauma and Compositional Engagement

In this chapter, Cassandra Lo will examine how rhetorical situations allow spaces for writing and thinking about personal traumas and how teachers can support this work. While some teachers are careful to avoid traumatic topics in their classrooms, writing assignments that provide students with a choice of topic or form can invite them, while not requiring or expecting them, to share testimonials of trauma. Trauma writing and personal narratives can offer critical counternarratives to preexisting stories about both communities and individuals scripted by the dominant culture. In-class writing activities are invitations for students to share from their lived experiences; furthermore, they represent spaces where students can share testimonials of trauma and witness other students' testimonials. Post-writing activities can support community-building efforts and provide a space for students to share their traumatic writing. Mindfulness and embodied writing activities, shared by Kristen Park Wedlock, can also be implemented after students write and share on difficult topics. This chapter will discuss pre- and post-writing activities that encourage testimony and witness.

> You own everything that happened to you. Tell your stories.
> — Anne Lamott, *Bird by Bird: Some Instructions on Writing and Life*

During my first year of teaching, I tried to think about ways to engage my eleventh graders in the college essay writing process. As a warm-up activity for the essay, I researched supplemental essay prompts from college applications across the US, and I put those prompts into a brainstorming questionnaire to help the students come up with topics for their essays. One question read, "If your house was infested by termites, and you could only grab one possession on the way out, what would you take?" The class worked diligently to complete the handout. I asked for students to share responses if they felt comfortable. When we got to the termite question, one student's hand shot up quickly. I was expecting answers such as a favorite gaming system, money, or even family heirlooms, but this student's answer surprised me. "I would take my brother, because he has autism and wouldn't know how to get out of the house."

The responses to this questionnaire and Peter's college essay draft (details can be found in chapter 4) led me to deeply examine my pedagogy and to rethink which writing genres I had privileged in my classroom previously. I was determined to include personal narrative writing through informal, low-stakes activities and more high-stakes assignments over the course of the year to help students become more comfortable with the genre and with sharing about themselves. These activities fostered relationships within the classroom, as students formed bonds through what they shared, and also provided a space for students to write and share testimonials of trauma (Dutro, 2019; Felman and Laub, 1992). Sharing personal narratives and storytelling through writing and sharing activities can be healing for students who have experienced trauma if the classroom is not a hostile space and if teachers approach assignments and activities with care.

Personal Writing about Trauma

Personal writing has been both shunned and celebrated over the past forty years, but as the number of standardized tests administered to students rises, the personal writing genre is being replaced by formulaic essay responses that can prepare students for these exams. Yagelski (2009) highlights the omission of personal writing from current curricula because of the necessity of preparing for standardized writing assessments that require compositions to fall into the expository or argumentative categories. He argues, "[S]chool-sponsored writing is about separating self from experience by changing an experience into a stylized textual artifact" (p.19). Current writing instruction for standardized tests encourages formulaic, five-paragraph essays that follow a very specific structure. Even if students are able to incorporate their own experience, relegated to certain paragraphs throughout the essay, and their experience often has to be deemed a "worthy" type of experience. Herrington (2002) believes, "[W]e should value students being able to bring their own authoritative knowledge from personal experience into academic writing, not as inferior to formalized theory and knowledge, but as equal" (238). Teachers are still privileging traditional composition genres, including expository essays, research assignments, and persuasive writing, over personal writing in the classroom because they feel pressure for their students to succeed on standardized tests.

Omitting personal writing from middle and high school classrooms perpetuates the common misconception that it is not as "important" as other genres. As Kamler (2001) states, "I am also dissatisfied with current competency-based moves to eradicate the personal from school writing altogether and focus on the more functional genres students need to master in the 'real world'" (1). This de-emphasis of personal writing deprives students of a necessary outlet for expression and healing: "Missing from many adolescents' schooling experiences are opportunities for their expressive practices and narratives to be nurtured, and to be recognized as people with 'personal and powerful' stories to share with multiple and varying audiences" (Stornaiuolo, Hull, and Nelson, 2009, as cited in Wissman and Vasudevan, 2012). There is a clear disconnect between the goals of policymakers and the needs of students; consequently, students' voices are rarely heard in discussions on curricular development or standards creation.

In contrast to the devaluing of personal writing, the Common Application for United States colleges and universities expects students to write deeply personal essays that share about their (often traumatic) life experiences in order to be accepted. Warren (2013) cites a statistic from a 2011 survey by the National Association for College Admissions Counseling that states sixty percent of four-year colleges surveyed placed "considerable importance" or "moderate importance" on the college essay. Because of this emphasis, the college essay is arguably the most high-stakes essay a student will have to write during their K–12 schooling. Affluent students have the ability to employ tutors and seek extra support in the writing of this essay as well as seek counseling for emotional support; on the other hand, Early, DeCosta-Smith, and Valdespino (2010) point out that students from low-income, underrepresented groups do not always have the ability to receive similar supports. These students must rely on in-school resources for guidance and support when crafting their college essays. Although these high-stakes essays are expected to be reflective and masterfully crafted, there is no space in English language arts curricula for teachers to share personal writing strategies or witness their students' stories.

As students select experiences to write about, traumatic moments often surface, as the prompts lend themselves to deep personal reflection and remembrance. Paley (1996) calls the college admission essay a test of "emotional literacy" that forces students to divulge information about themselves to an anonymous committee of readers who are judging their experiences. Carello and Butler (2015) write, "[S]tudents may push their own emotional limits in an effort to please the instructor or to excel in the assignment" (271). Students unfortunately assume that if they divulge their deeply personal moments, they will be more likely to be accepted to a university, or their teachers will be pleased with their choice. Their assumption is understandable when we begin to consider the essay topics that students can choose to write about for their college admissions essays. Following are the 2021–2022 Common Application prompts:

Common Application Essay Prompts

1. Some students have a background, identity, interest, or talent that is so meaningful they believe their application would be incomplete without it. If this sounds like you, then please share your story.
2. The lessons we take from obstacles we encounter can be fundamental to later success. Recount a time when you faced a challenge, setback, or failure. How did it affect you, and what did you learn from the experience?
3. Reflect on a time when you questioned or challenged a belief or idea. What prompted your thinking? What was the outcome?
4. Reflect on something that someone has done for you that has made you happy or thankful in a surprising way. How has this gratitude affected or motivated you?
5. Discuss an accomplishment, event, or realization that sparked a period of personal growth and a new understanding of yourself or others.
6. Describe a topic, idea, or concept you find so engaging that it makes you lose all track of time. Why does it captivate you? What or who do you turn to learn more?
7. Share an essay on any topic of your choice. It can be one you've already written, one that responds to a different prompt, or one of your own design.

It is clear that the Common Application is almost requiring students to provide deeply personal information in order to complete a "successful" essay. Students struggle with whether to disclose information about their past, including their medical history or disabilities, that are essential parts of their life story but could negatively impact their chances at being admitted, despite the claims from universities that these essays will be evaluated by unbiased readers (Vidali, 2007). Over the past ten years, the prompts have remained very similar with a variety of suggestions asking students to recall events from their past that have shaped them into who they are today. Unfortunately, regardless of the intent of the universities that require essays, assigning these prompts to students fails to consider the consequences of students going through the process of writing about traumatic moments without much support or guidance.

The college essay is not the only time when trauma writing emerges in classrooms, but there are few opportunities in today's secondary English classrooms for students to share about difficult topics. Trauma writing, when implemented carefully, can be a healing and cathartic practice for students. Trauma writing serves as a "testimonial" (Felman and Laub, 1992) of a student's experiences and can be a part of small-scale writing activities or larger projects. An empirical study by Dr. Elizabeth Dutro (2011), professor of education at the University of Colorado Boulder and one of the prominent voices in the discussion about trauma and literacy in schools, shows the importance of allowing students to write while "wounded." Dutro begins her article, "Writing Wounded: Trauma, Testimony, and Critical Witness in Literacy Classrooms," by arguing, "[E]motions are part and parcel of literature study and of classroom life and too often bracketed from our notions of what constitutes an education or a curriculum" (3). She argues that personal writing finds its way into the classroom through informal daily activities without even a formal personal writing assignment. Dutro pushes back against the critiques of personal writing by stating that writing about trauma eliminates the deficit perspectives often surrounding children in urban schools. Dutro writes:

> I turn to difficult experiences as one way to challenge such Othering. I want to consider the potential of such experiences to serve as a resource for building the kinds of visceral connections—and awareness of disconnections—that call into question the impulse to speak as though we know about a life or an entire community of lives, when all we know is the façade that has been narrated and re-narrated in the image and voice of the materially privileged. (7)

By allowing her students to write through traumatic moments, they wrote their own life stories. When underrepresented people are not the ones telling their own stories, "Othering" and incomplete stories are shared. Trauma writing and personal narratives offer critical counternarratives to preexisting stories about both communities and individuals scripted by the dominant culture. Dutro utilizes trauma studies to examine the compositional happenings in her classroom as an elementary teacher and the classrooms she observed as a researcher. She found that "testimony and witness in classrooms . . . was not a linear, uni-dimensional process, but rather was circular and cyclical . . . it implies that there is not a point of leveling off and being 'done'" (9). This relates to Lensmire's (2000) "voice as project" proposal because the writing/revising/rewriting process of personal writing is most beneficial when it is cyclical and recurring. Just as our lives are ever changing, Dutro notes that her students' stories are as well. Feedback from both teachers and peers helps encourage students to continue working through the writing cycle and thinking reflectively about their lived experiences.

Critical and Reciprocal Witnessing

Personal writing allows for a connection that would not surface otherwise, because allowing students to write from personal experience often produces a connection of wounds. The notion of witnessing found in trauma studies can be taken a step further in schools by promoting and supporting "critical witnessing" and reciprocal witnessing in the classroom, both of which are deeper ways to connect when participants share lived experiences and memories that are surfaced by either texts or conversation (Dutro, 2008; Dutro, 2017; Zembylas, 2006). This type of interaction also affirms a student's experience in ways that traditional listening does not because it involves connecting and relationships. Dutro (2011) shares her observation of connectivity in her classes: "In literacy classrooms, I posit, this sharing of our students' wounds demands us to awaken to the ways our stories are connected to those we witness. At the same time, those connections must be allowed to reveal the potentially different ways that we and our students are positioned by our challenges" (11). Within the model of critical witnessing, personal writing becomes communal writing that engenders critical conversations about privilege and power. Dutro (2009) emphasizes that "critical witnessing requires awareness of the assumptions educators bring to their interpretations of students' lives" (236). The explanation of the tension that occurs through critical witnessing is a direct counter to the argument that teachers cannot relate to traumas they have not experienced (Alexander, 2004; Wissman and Wiseman, 2011). This practice is accomplished when teachers listen and internalize the information about their students' identities. It is especially valuable for teachers who do not share identities with their students. According to the National Center for Education Statistics, in the 2017–2018 school year, about seventy-nine percent of K–12 public school teachers in the US identified as White and seventy-six percent identified as female. There is a high likelihood that teachers will not share all identities with their students, which is why it is important for teachers to find ways to truly listen to, hear, and support *all* of their students. If teachers are able to engage in critical witnessing and recognize the issues of race, class, gender, and numerous others that are pervasive in their classrooms, then classroom communities can be strengthened and improved.

Another important aspect of listening to testimonials of trauma within the classroom is reciprocal witnessing. The act of reciprocal witnessing brings about an understanding between participants, as testimonials of trauma are shared reciprocally, and deeper relationships are forged. This shared experience helps to reduce the possible Othering and alienation that can occur when students share their testimonies of trauma without any reciprocal sharing: "A teacher's testimony to difficult experiences does not happen every day, but it does need to happen early and periodically as reminders to children that all aspects of life are valued as resources in this classroom" (Dutro, 2017, 333). Dutro argues that this type of relationship will help to build trust, and that trust should not just be assumed since teachers and support staff members are the adults in authority positions at a school. Reciprocal witnessing does not demand full similarity between testimonials, but rather it can serve as a way to demonstrate to the person who shared a testimonial of trauma that they are not alone in their experiences.

Forging relationships between teachers and students, as well as encouraging relationships among students within a classroom community, can aid in support through listening and sharing. Within these classroom communities "survival and bearing witness become reciprocal acts" (Des Pres, 1980, as cited in Felman and Laub, 1992). Christie et al. (2016) write about a reciprocal witnessing workshop for adolescents who experienced chronic pain that took place in a hospital. According to participants, this reciprocal witnessing workshop resulted in an increased ability to discuss the emotions surrounding a patient's trauma. It also resulted in patients being able to meet and discuss their circumstances with others who understood (Christie et al., 2016). Reciprocal witnessing is often shared through storytelling, both oral and written stories, and can enter a classroom through literacy practices, assignments, or activities. The activities discussed below can allow students to practice their personal writing skills while also inviting (but not requiring) students to write testimonials of trauma and bearing witness to others' testimonials. They challenge the traditional norms of "call and response" classroom teaching and center students' voices and experiences.

Creating Class Expectations

Before my students began writing and sharing in class, I asked them to create a list of expectations they had for themselves, for their classmates, and for me. We created this list collaboratively, and each class had a slightly different list. Unsurprisingly, the classes prioritized similar things. Here is a list of expectations from one group of students:

1. *Try participating in each activity, but you do not have to share aloud if you feel uncomfortable.*
2. *Please allow for "wait time" after someone speaks in case they need to finish.*
3. *It is okay to share emotions.*
4. *Please do not laugh when someone else is sharing their story.*

I specifically chose to call these points a list of "expectations" instead of "rules" because of the disciplinary nature of the word "rules." These were goals we all had for ourselves and our fellow group members as we began to build our community. This practice is helpful for all practitioners in order to create a foundation of understanding amongst classmates. I referred back to these expectations each time we engaged in a personal writing exercise and occasionally asked the class if they'd like to alter or add any. The addition of point four—*Please do not laugh when someone else is sharing their story*—by the students was one they returned to often. I worked with this particular group of students while completing my dissertation at the University of Pennsylvania. These students attended an all-boys' school in a large Northeast city. A majority of students at the school identified as Black or African American. When the students created this list of expectations, they mentioned moments of taunting and rejection from their peers that crippled their ability to share and speak freely in the past. With these expectations set forth early in the school year, we were able to begin writing and sharing with less hesitation. Of course, these written expectations did not necessarily put the students completely at ease, but I found that being upfront and collaborative about what we were all planning on doing together served as an effective method of community building.

Prewriting Activity: Artifact Exchange

This prewriting activity was adapted from a National Writing Project professional development activity I attended in 2012 when I was a high school teacher. On the day of the assignment, students should bring an artifact, or object of significance, from home that has meaning to them. This artifact can be anything from clothing to collectables to toys, but I always warned students to not bring in anything incredibly valuable, as they pass their artifact to another student during this activity. The artifact exchange has four different layers of storytelling, all focusing on the artifact. First, students exchange their artifacts with a peer and spend two minutes writing about just the physical appearance of the new artifact. Then, they spend five minutes writing a story about what they think the significance of the object might be. Next, the students receive their original artifact back and spend five minutes writing about its actual significance. Finally, they share both their story from step two and the story of their actual artifact with their partner. I also invite students to share their responses with the whole class at this time.

One year during the activity, one student proudly showed off his father's bottle of cologne and told us that he was now the owner of his father's cologne collection since his father had passed away. Another student brought in a bracelet from their community pool to represent the moment they overcame their fear of water. I shared a sewing kit my late grandmother put together for me when I went off to college. I shared the sewing kit one year after my grandmother passed, and my grief was still raw. My partner student wrote a beautiful story about how my grandmother had passed on this sewing kit to me because I was her favorite granddaughter. I felt a sense of pride rush over me as I heard my student share their version of my story. This activity provided students (and me) with a place to discuss their keepsakes and allowed them to share something of importance from their lives. I always included a post-exercise reflection in which I asked students to debrief about the activity. During this period, the students mentioned that this activity helped them get to know each other better. It is a valuable activity to do at the beginning of the school year when the classroom community is being built. Students in my classes often used these objects as inspiration for their college essays or longer personal writing assignments later in the school year.

Post-writing Activity: Quaker Reading

A Quaker reading is a post-writing activity that can both build community and build confidence in individual writers. Quaker pedagogy is student-centered and challenges the traditional notion of the teacher as the focus of feedback and classroom discussion (Johnson, 2002). For this practice, readers identify key parts of another person's work and then share it aloud. Students are encouraged to share any parts that resonate with them, even if they are repeated by another student. What results is a chorus of lines from every student's work, letting them know that their work is meaningful to a classmate.

For this exercise, students submit a writing piece to a shared document that all classmates have access to. It is important to explain the activity to students before they write, so they are aware they will be sharing their writing with the class. Once the class collection is complete, each student is given access to it, either in print or digitally. The students read and annotate each piece, underlining lines that are most powerful to them. I encourage students to underline at least one line from each classmate's work. During the actual Quaker reading, students are asked to share aloud the lines that spoke to them from their classmates' work when they feel ready to share. There is no order to the sharing—students call out at any time. Students are encouraged to repeat quotes that others have shared already if they also find them moving, because that shows the true power of their peers' words. This activity can go on until there are long silences between lines. I try to make sure each student's writing has been shared at least once before the activity ends. Hearing writing shared by a classmate is an important experience for students, as it shows that their work is impactful to an audience. As the teacher, seeing their positive reactions as their words are shared is a special moment.

After the activity, I again asked students to reflect. Students shared why they selected certain lines from their classmates' work. This reflection period was when a significant amount of reciprocal witnessing occurred. Often, these explanations become new testimonials that students feel comfortable sharing because a peer has shared. The connection they felt to the lines they read aloud often formed because it reminded them of their own experiences. One student wrote about the day their father passed away, and a line was shared from their essay: "But then one day he did not show up." Another student shared this line and also shared that they, too, lost their father and had a similar experience of feeling like their father had disappeared. Beyond personal writing, this activity can be done with lines from a book or a poem as well and sometimes serves as an easier way for students to discuss their own experiences, since they are comparing it to another previously existing thought.

Mindfulness Practices to Support Testimony and Witness

I worked closely with a school psychologist when I created my dissertation study in 2016. This psychologist had run a grief support group for students at the high school where I had taught who had lost family members. Over the years, my students who had lost parents or siblings would miss class to attend this important group. Some of them would stop by afterward to catch up on missed work and describe the group meeting. The students shared that the community aspect of the group meeting was most important for them, because they got to know other students in school who were experiencing loss. The school psychologist told me that the most difficult part of the group was wrapping up the conversation at the end of the period. A forty-minute block can fly by in a minute when deep conversations occur. How can students shift their thoughts from grief to algebra at the ring of a bell? If teachers plan to engage their students in narrative writing activities that may lead to testimony and witness in their classrooms, they should also plan to incorporate mindfulness exercises. Below, Kristen shares contemplative and mindful activities that can set the tone for a supportive classroom community.

Contemplative Pedagogy: The Apple of my i/I/eye

When designing lessons using contemplative pedagogy, the experience is scaffolded to include nothingness (no-thing-ness), awareness, discernment, and contemplation (Barbezat and Bush, 2014). As a writing instructor, I think about this in terms of the beholding/reading/sitting we do with our prompts/materials/assignments (nothingness), the divergent brainstorming/prewriting we use to explore and discover possibilities (awareness), the outlining/planning we engage in to create a focus, structure, and container for our words (discernment), and the drafting/revising/writing we practice to unpack, dismantle, negotiate, process, and experience our subject (contemplation). I share here my favorite first-day-of-class activity that demonstrates this pedagogical style.

Preparation: Grab enough apples for each student in your class. Get some Grannies and some Macs and some Pink Ladies—a variety in color, flavor, size, and texture is key. Wash and dry. Place each apple in a brown lunch bag and fold down. (I have done this with oranges in February [investigating your navel] and pears in the summer [don't try this—the skin ripens in the brown bag! Messy!) and even different herbs [when I taught at a culinary school]). This semester, during the pandemic, I will try the exercise with flowers—nothing edible. Put all of the brown bags in one big shopping bag—build the mystery.

Nothingness: Walk up and down the rows, instructing your students to reach in and grab a bag—and to not open it but to let it sit on the desk in front of them. Prompt: *There is a bag on the desk in front of you and you don't know what it holds inside. Sit with this uncertainty.*

Awareness: We will make a little joke about kindergarten and the five senses to break the mystery object tension, so I write on the board the senses. Students share popcorn-style ways of perceiving sound, touch, smell, taste, and sight, and I jot these up as a shared criteria/language for exploring our mystery objects. *Prompt: With your eyes closed (or glancing at the floor next to you if closing your eyes makes you feel unsafe), listen to the sound the object makes . . . in motion . . . when still . . . in contrast to its container. . . . Write on your page: I hear . . . list all the descriptors of sound that you notice when listening to the mystery object.* We continue the exercise to include *I feel* (with my hands not my heart), *I smell* (with ellipses, not a period), *I taste*, and at the end, *I see.* This constitutes the field notes of our experience; we have practiced observational attention. When the focus shifts from what is happening here and now with the object in front of us, we bring the attention back. Back to the bag, to the object, to the mystery.

Discernment: After the students collect all the observations—the concrete, the descriptors—they then return to the notes to practice discernment. *Prompt: Sift through your list in each sense category and select the top one or two observations in each. What are you drawn to? Circle them. Then, identify the two sense categories that best distinguish your object from all the other objects like it and all the other encounters you may have had with an object "like" this.*

Discussion: I then launch into a mini-lesson on concrete versus abstract language, leaning on the poet, William Carlos Williams: "there is no truth but in things." We unpack the coding—the linguistic baggage of APPLE—as it exists in our shared world: apple of my eye (apple as good); one bad apple spoils the bunch (apple as bad); apple doesn't fall far from the tree (apple as family/ seed/ line); Adam and Eve's apple (apple as temptation); an apple a day keeps the doctor away (apple as health); Snow White's apple (apple as beauty/temptation); iMac (Apple as computer/brand); apple bottom jeans, boots with fur (apple as desire/temptation);

Johnny Appleseed (apples spreading seed); and, of course, an apple for the teacher (apple as appreciation/learning/fall/school). The apple is a symbol, and so it carries through language the story of all the other apples that came before and the expectation of all GOOD apples to follow. As will be described in detail in chapter 9, the default mode network in our brains allows us to attend to the REAL apple (on the desk, in front of us) and the IDEAL apple (the stories of all the apples in the past and the desires for all apples in the future). This subtle priming of bringing our attention to the REAL apple—experiential focus—can help our students develop active listening and close reading skills as well as cultivate intellectual humility and awareness of bias. (For the science on how this works, turn to chapter 9.) While we want our students to access their abstract thought and narrative capabilities (narrative focus), we want them to do this with a grounded and authentic approach instead of a habitual reaching for the nearest script: IDEAL apples are red, shiny, sweet, crisp, and smooth; they are GOOD, KIND, SMART, DEPENDABLE "fruits."

Contemplation: In contemplation we sit with both all the apples and this apple. What questions, words, sensations, feelings, memories, thoughts arise as we hold the space? *Prompt: Using your field notes from the senses exercise, your awareness of the other apples in this room, and your knowledge of apples, create a one-to-three line description of your apple here and now. How could we pick out your apple in a barrel of apples based on this description?*

Sharing: Then we go around the room listening to the Apple Prose-Poems (awareness) and identifying which senses are engaged (discernment) and considering what we can learn about both this apple and about the person experiencing the apple (contemplation). The observational attention cycles again in holding the shared space (see the Kerr et al. [2011] study in chapter 9).

So, why talk about apples and language and attention in the context of trauma literacy? Inviting mindfulness exercises into the classroom requires the building of trust (chapter 4), and trauma survivors may grapple with their right to be "here" (chapter 3 and chapter 8). While many mindfulness cues start with the body as the subject—the breath and the pulse—the body in trauma can be uncoupled from a sense of self, creating a stage of overwhelm in the nervous system. The traumatized body can become the objectified body when left unacknowledged. In a time where collective trauma is finally being given the attention it deserves, this feels like an important first step in the trust-building process.

Language can carry stories—archetypes, metaphors, symbols, myths, warnings—and thus transmit knowledge over time. While comparative and categorical thinking are essential components of critical thinking, we offer here the balance of discernment with awareness as a method for confronting the labels, stereotypes, and generalizations encoded in words. During trauma, the survivor's Broca area—speech—oftentimes shuts down (chapter 3); in a culture that privileges speech as effective communication, the trauma survivor can become alienated from themselves and others unable to "make people understand" or to "find the right words." Mindfulness exercises and embodied writing bring an attitude of nonstriving and nonjudgment to language. Providing students with opportunities to practice mediating experiential focus and narrative focus can liberate the current self—this apple, in this bunch, at this time—from all the expectations or memories of what an apple should, could, might be: what a student should, could, might be.

This small, low-stakes activity can serve as an introduction to contemplative pedagogy and mindfulness in the English classroom.

Focused Attention and Open Monitoring: Mindfulness in the Body and on the Page

In Buddhist texts and MBSR (see chapter 9) protocols, mindfulness starts in the body and with the breath. I have adopted the Body Scan (Jon Kabbat-Zinn's version), as a way to instruct attentional focus (build observational awareness) and have used the Body Story as a way to introduce embodied writing to the English classroom. The Body Scan starts with the prompt to *feel the inside edge of your left big toe, and then feel the outside edge of your little toe, and then feel all the toes in between. Inhale your breath into the toe, then exhale, feel it leave the toe.*

Directing the attention to the breath and then moving the breath through the body in a way that is on purpose and without judgment allows participants to explore their body and mind: their relationship to self. How does the mind react or respond to the focus: attraction, aversion; nonjudgment, attachment; focused, wandering; etc.? What sensations, thoughts, or feelings arise as one moves the breath through the body? After the Body Scan, students excavate their experience—their field notes—for a story that the body-mind wants to show the self: Where, when, how, and on what did your attention wander or linger in the scan?

In the Body Story, students are invited to write about a scar—physical, emotional, mental, spiritual, or psychic—that came up during the Body Scan. What stories and in what language have we been told about our bodies? What stories have we constructed or created about our own bodies, and what stories have others constructed or created for our bodies? What language has been used to label our flesh, to mark our minds, and to transmit social and sexual norms? Who was doing the speaking and what power or authority did they have over us? When we talk, think, feel, or sense our bodies, what words arrive and where do they resist, split, break, reach, puncture, or exorcise? Do we see ourselves as an individual or part of a community, a collective, or a family body? For survivors of trauma, this exercise can be an opportunity to explore and share their story, or it can become a deterrent—resistance as protection—just as we saw in previous chapters. (See chapter 7 and chapter 8 for scaffolding and assessing this assignment. The exercises in chapter 10 center resources and support for instructors as they navigate trauma in the English classroom.)

Whereas in the apple exercise, the object of attention was outside of the body, in the Body Scan, the object of attention is the body. In open-monitoring exercises, the attention rests not on an object but rather sits back and watches the thoughts, feelings, sensations as they arise. This type of insight meditation comes from the Vipassana tradition in Buddhism. (For more on open monitoring, see chapter 10.) Here, we will share how open monitoring can be practiced on the page.

The page becomes a site for recording the experience and thus becomes a text that can be read: patterns discerned, habits explored, and bias confronted. Both Allen Ginsberg in *Mind Writing Slogans* and Jack Kerouac in *Essentials of Spontaneous Prose* herald the benefits of automatic writing. Composition classrooms call this "freewriting" or "quickwrites": a time limit is set, and the prompt to not filter, edit, or think is shared. The difference between the practices lies in the intention. Unlike freewrites and quickwrites, there is no defined outcome or expectation (even brainstorming implies that an idea will arrive). This attitude of nonstriving is not inherently compatible with Western education in which lesson plans have goals, objectives, and outcomes aligned for each activity. This writing is pure play, watch, observe, attend for the sake of playing, watching, observing, and attending.

What we advocate here is that when practiced regularly—disciplined interiority—participants show higher levels of curiosity, resilience, creativity, metacognition, and metareflection (see chapter 9). This practice also supports the idea that writing is not just a process but is also a way of processing. Through writing, one can come to understand what they are studying and to be accepting of what they still do not understand (aka every line in a poem). For our survivors of trauma, the neuroplasticity this exercise invokes, and thus the physical, mental, and emotional resilience it creates, can be more accessible and desirable than efforts to build self-awareness through speech.

Whether it is setting the tone of the class at the beginning of the semester (apple exercise), creating spaces for students to share their identities (personal artifact writing), inviting embodied voices into the classroom (Body Scan / Story), participating in reciprocal witnessing to build a community (Quaker-style sharing), or opening or concluding a class with insight meditation (one or two minutes of open-monitoring writing), mindfulness exercises support trauma literacy for students and instructors.

Conclusion

Critical and reciprocal witnessing involve a deeper understanding between students and teachers, and students and other students, especially about testimonials of trauma. This type of interaction also affirms a student's experience in ways that traditional listening does not because it involves connecting and relationships. Having students and teachers share in the same way provides a level playing field for interaction in the classroom. One of the main reasons teachers don't want to present moments of vulnerability, however, is because they don't want to get too close to their students or make their classroom an emotional space, but Kinloch (2010) argues that both teachers and students must take risks in order to get to know each other through literacy encounters. Critical and reciprocal witnessing are also a factor of what Winn (2013) calls restorative English education. This type of education "seeks to restore classrooms and schools into peacemaking and peacekeeping spaces where students learn empathy as well as how to build healthy relationships through learning about themselves and each other" (132–133).

Restorative English education provides a way for students who have been marginalized both in classrooms and in society to rejoin a classroom community. Winn cautions teachers to not confuse restorative education with "safe spaces," however, which can never be guaranteed because classrooms cannot be truly confidential places. Chapter 4 discussed the need for a relational approach within classrooms that features personal narrative writing and provided some suggestions for how to foster relationships in the classroom. In chapters 7 and 8, we think about how these activities and assignments can be assessed and how grades can acknowledge risk-taking in writing. Activities and assignments pertaining to trauma writing do not simply occur in a vacuum; they need to be supported beforehand and afterward in order to be the most successful and meaningful for students.

All of the activities mentioned here can foster a space for testimony and witness and can invite students to share about instances of trauma. At the same time, they can provide a significant amount of choice in levels of sharing. Students get to choose what they bring to class or what they write about, and they also choose if they want to share with their classmates. By offering exercises and activities like the ones discussed previously, students can begin to gain comfort in writing about difficult topics, and they can build relationships with their peers and their teacher as they witness each other's testimonials. These powerful practices enrich a classroom community and provide space for our students' authentic stories to be heard.

Chapter 6: Questions for Reflection

1. How can you support your students as they compose personal writing assignments? How can you affirm their stories while also providing important constructive feedback?
2. Considering the exercises presented in this chapter, are there any that you feel can be implemented in your classroom? Are there any adjustments you can make to better accommodate your students?
3. Crying is most associated with sharing deep personal stories, but laughter is also just as common in the classroom. When we invite students to express themselves, emotion moves through the body, page, and the classroom. How can we explore with our students what these "bursts" (or "outbursts") of expression mean in the context of writing, sharing, and processing stories? When entering new territory in the classroom, how do you debrief these bursts of expression with your students? Is there room?
4. Those who have unprocessed or unacknowledged trauma often feel like they are "out of control" or "do not have a say." These exercises balance instruction with choice. In which stages of the writing process can you offer choices to your students? What would that look or sound like in one of your assignments or activities?

7

Responding to and Assessing Student Writing

Trauma disrupts, disorients, and displaces; it makes a mess. When trauma shows up in the drafting process, it does not spare the page. In this chapter, Kristen Park Wedlock and Cassandra Lo explore how to approach, embrace, and respond to the messy pages students share when drafting, revising, and submitting written work. Both writing center and composition pedagogues warn against "fixing the writing." In the case of trauma-informed writing pedagogy, this "don't fix the writing" mantra also includes "don't fix the writer." Tidying up the page does not actually help writers process the complex intellectual, emotional, and social truths that trauma is forcing them to confront. In fact, it can come across as an act of erasure, silence, and oppression. Strategies from narratology, experimental prose, and contemplative poetics for engaging with student work are offered as alternatives. By sharing examples of instructor feedback and risk-inclusive rubrics, this chapter navigates the uncertain terrain of formative and summative assessment in student trauma writing.

> Instead of teaching finished writing, we should teach unfinished writing, and glory in its unfinishedness. We work with language in action.
>
> — Donald Murray, "Teach Writing as a Process Not Product"

At the end of my (Cassie's) first year teaching eleventh grade, I assigned the college essay. I was confident that I knew what my students would be writing about, since I had spent eight months building relationships with them. The first essay was about a father who was murdered. The second was about a brother who was profoundly impacted by autism. These parts of my students' lives were silenced in school. I grappled with how to grade an essay of this magnitude. As students submitted applications during senior year, this narrative carried a significant weight. If students were rejected, they began to doubt their writing skills, and some believed that the story they shared caused the rejection. They entered college as students who lacked self-confidence in their writing and who lacked the confidence to share their true selves in a classroom setting.

I (Kristen) leaned against the doorframe as my EN101 students handed over their first rough drafts of the semester; my "thank yous" were met with diverted eyes and sweaty corner-folded submissions. The last paper had a note attached—longer than the draft—full of apology, fear, and hope. The urge to protect these pages, these voices, overwhelmed me. I clutched the stack to my chest. I asked for this—honesty, authenticity, creativity in the guise of sensory description, symbols, open letters, vignette meditations, visceral testimony, and flashbacks—and now, I held it in my hands. I had to respond, push, and eventually grade their writing.

It feels important to note that when I collect stacks of expository or literary analysis or even argument papers, there is no desperate clutching, diving, slipping, or spilling, even though their ideas are just as raw and formulating, just as new to the page. It is the personal narrative essay that elicits a visceral response in me. Where does the fear come from (on both our parts) and what drives it: judgment? Failure? Exposure? Incompetence? Memory? Intimacy? Uncertainty? And is it "fear" or something else?

The day they flipped through the assignment in my academic and research writing class—a prompt that encouraged them to explore the connection between language, memory, and identity through description, narrative, and reflection—I found myself, as a new instructor, on the other side of the cringe. "Well, what do you mean? Just tell me what you want me to write about" and the all-famous "how many paragraphs/words/pages should this be?" Why had I not considered these questions before (I as a student may have even asked them!)? But now I stood there in the front of the room and felt responsible for honoring my assignment and supporting my students as we stepped outside the traditional five-paragraph essay through which they had been indoctrinated into writing.

Long before the "assignment" had stood between us, we read Stephen Graham Jones "The Exodus," Joan Didion's "On Keeping a Notebook," Maxine Hong Kingston's "Tongue-Tied," Margaret Atwood's "The Female Body," and Langston Hughes's "Salvation." I grabbed onto the models and held them up as half-shield and half-mirror: "Well, what did the authors we read write about?"

"So, you want me to write about crabs, drugs, falling off the roof, losing my virginity, disappointing my parents, hating school, Barbie dolls, having my heart broken, losing faith in God, patriarchy, and notebooks?"

The part of me without tenure took a big, terrified breath, and the rest of me carried on: "YES."

The follow-up questions were just as valid and necessary: "But those are not essays, are they?"; "That guy doesn't even have an introduction paragraph"; "That one just rambles on like I am in her head"; "That one has, like, twenty-one paragraphs with numbers; do you want me to write twenty-one paragraphs with numbers?"

It got easier to just keep saying "YES," and the yes became more confident and powerful, and before long we were back to laughing at the big yes free-for-all we had just shared (as improv artists would say, the "yes, and" moment).

When the room quieted, I ran through my creative nonfiction platitudes in my head—*just let the writing happen, the writing will determine the form, write to the edge of it*—but I said out loud, to my own surprise and theirs: "Do you trust me?"

It was the first time they really looked at me—we had just spent four sessions eating apples, observing roommates, interviewing strangers, and discussing how cool the verb "splinter" is in Kingston's "Tongue Tied" (I can *see* it, *hear* it, and *feel* it happening)—some of them jumped on the YES bandwagon, but others, understandably, kept silent.

This was the moment when as an instructor I realized vulnerability was what we were sharing, and risk, play, and authenticity was what I was asking for. And trust—trust in me, in themselves, and in each other—would be the only way to hold the space for this exploration. How open or closed must the assignment be to prompt risk-taking? How flexible or rigid must the boundaries of the container be to encourage play and participation? How might my presence in the classroom, in the margins, and as a reader contribute to the perception of and expectations for the experience?

The therapeutic value of writing has not been lost on me. As a writer who uses contemplative poetics, somatic archeology, and movement arts to shape her practice, I am no stranger to writing about, through, with, and in trauma. Violence and grief rewrite the line—saplings in stone—rupturing, puncturing, flattening, dividing, suturing, scaffolding, and yes, splintering possible truths, probable truths, and authentic truths. But this is composition class, not therapy, and I am the writing instructor, not the therapist. I had embodied the value of experimental prose in building a relationship and conversation with trauma, and I wanted to offer this to my students: an invitation to this space, however murky and barbed.

Fortunately, I am not the first writing instructor to ever ask their students to write a personal narrative essay. And while it has been in and out of vogue in composition courses, I felt confident there was a literature review out there ready to ease my worries (see chapter 6).

Gun violence, global pandemics, police brutality, weather events, border disputes, cyberstalking, hate crimes, mass incarceration, body shaming, food insecurity, drug abuse: these "issues" become sites of atrocity marked in the bodies, hearts, and minds of American teens. In a landscape of roadside memorials, how do we excavate through writing the trauma that our students share *and* how do we as instructors of writing hold the space for critical witnessing and authentic counternarratives?

When I stood in that doorframe and felt the weight of their papers in my arms, it became clear: the door as threshold, the frame as protection—something to lean on and push through and notice—passed and passing. If writing is to be used to excavate memories, practice identities, process experiences, and challenge thoughts, then it is our responsibility as instructors to build this transom. What materials are essential for constructing a curatorial space for trauma, vulnerability, trust, and risk? And how do we begin?

This chapter explores the ways trust and truth, uncertainty and fear, vulnerability and receptivity, and risk and play enter the feedback and assessment of student writing. It matters both how and why we approach the page. How can we create rubrics and grade contracts that assess students while acknowledging their risks and providing constructive feedback to build their self-confidence as writers?

Formative Assessment: Feedback on the Rough Draft

While Anne Lamont invites writers to sift the silt of messy drafts for word gold, Donald Murray (1972) reminds instructors to welcome those drafts into the classroom: "Instead of teaching finished writing, we should teach unfinished writing, and glory in its unfinishedness. We work with language in action" (4). When we apply these recommendations to writing about or in trauma, the "finished" and "unfinished" take on new meaning. The mess—the words dropping, themes emerging, and structure forming—reveal clues not just about the relationship of word to word but also the relationship of writer to the words, and thus, the trauma they carry in them.

Saying that people experience trauma differently is a given; however, there are some patterns that are detectable in the way it shows up in the writing and their approach to the writing. A traumatic event not only interrupts the life of the person (chapter 3), but it also disrupts the narrative the person carries on about themselves (chapter 9). The body is jarred; the mind jarred; the story jarred up. When we tell the writer to open the jar and dip in the sharp edge of their pen, neither instructor nor writer can predict what will pour onto the page. When writers recall a traumatic event, they may find they have no memories at all—dissociating or blacking out, especially while in pain, in violation, or witnessing violence, is common. Other times, writers may find themselves in a sensory image overload—a vividness that shakes from the language of description into the somatic reckoning of their bodies. Both can leave the writer grasping for something that grounds or centers them back in the safe time (now) and the safe place (not there). If the writer finds themselves in either of these two poles, they may be at risk for retraumatizing themselves by writing about this event (chapters 2 and 3). Writing instructors must position themselves not to heal or serve or "fix" student trauma, but they must prepare themselves to recognize it and have a plan in place to get the student to the resources they need in the moment. Writing instructors are not therapists and should not take on this role.

Writing makes what is invisible visible through the act of representation. Over time and exposure, memory can crystallize the retrievable sensations, feelings, and thoughts—can create scar tissue over the event—to protect the traumatized from revisiting the experience. When the scar limits the range of motion—"language in action"—or conceals something essential, the person will not be speaking or living their truth: the body keeps secrets from the self, and the self keeps secrets from the body. These are the extremes—the all kinds of messy—and they manifest in and on the page with great variation. As writing and literacy instructors, we can learn to listen to the mess to hear the silence, the noise, and the voices as they breach the surface. Murray's "language in action" in the context of trauma prompts us to listen to how the writer delivers, arrives, postures, ruptures, reaches, falls, bends, and splits on the page.

John MacDevitt (2013), counselor and composition instructor, leverages his experience in both fields to apply the construct Karen Surman Paley and Salvador Minuchin, family therapists, offer about feedback relationships in the family to feedback relationships in the margins of composition papers:

> The parents in an enmeshed family may become quite upset when a child does not eat dessert. The parents in a disengaged family may not respond to a child's delinquent behavior. Responding only to problems with grammar and punctuation, she says, the instructor is at the disengaged end of the spectrum. Ignoring writing issues and only focusing on the pain and emotion—playing therapist—she places at the enmeshed end of the spectrum. (138)

In this section, we include the patterns we notice in writing with the motivations and desires of the storyteller (the writer/narrator/student) to ground the feedback in a healthy place on the continuum of disengaged and enmeshed. Reading narratives that contain trauma—*consuming* the literature of our students—requires support and tools to navigate their *declarations.* (An important note: student papers will not show up with a trigger warning. See chapter 10 for recommendations on preparing the instructor for sustainably practicing in this pedagogy.)

That very first stack of papers I clutched to my chest in guardianship contained drafts full of risk, revelation, and mess; they were beautiful and painful and authentic. I struggled with even knowing where to store them in my house, as I was living the adjunct life of car-trunk office hours. I had been trained first as a professional dancer, then as a cardiac and physical rehabilitation aide, and then as a somatic yoga practitioner to listen to the patterns in gestures, shapes, structures, postures, arrangements, and temporalities—to read the body, to use the body to write the line. During my graduate work in contemplative poetics at Naropa University, these skills were subsumed under the giant umbrella of "composition"—all this compiling and composing and composting had prepared me to hold these pages, these bodies of work. I just had to trust it. So, my students and I took a leap together.

The mess doesn't always mean what we might think it does—that they don't care or they don't know—but it is the indicator that something requires listening . . . to the static, to the debris, to put the story in a context: "Reentering past writing in this way allows students to dig deeper into ideas, initiating a more vertical movement in their writing processes. Past drafts become layers and turning points—with layers and turning points within them—all part of the longer story of the student's writing, learning, and growth" (Myers, 2016, 400). Butler and Carello (2015) note that one trauma-informed approach students appreciate is "nonjudgmental feedback on drafts," which allows them to write comfortably without the fear of repercussion (273). This models contemplative pedagogy (described in chapter 6): first no-thing-ness, then awareness, then discernment, and finally, contemplation. Reflecting back to the writer the themes emerging in the text, stating observations about what one notices in the text, and asking questions rather than doling out prescriptions frame Butler and Carello's (2015) trauma-informed approach in contemplative pedagogy to create a trauma-conscious feedback response.

The table below reflects the patterns collected from isolating, revisiting, and analyzing the messy rough drafts of reflection/personal essay/narrative assignments in composition classes and college admissions essays. While these observations can be made about both writing that does not reveal trauma and writing that does reveal trauma, the very presence—the context—of trauma alters the reading of the text, provides useful information about/to/for the writer, and changes the way in which feedback should be framed and delivered. Trauma occurs as a violation of the body-heart-mind (assault, abuse, injury, accident, addiction, and more), as a disruptive loss or deep grief (war, death, divorce, accident, disease, abandonment, neglect, and many others), as a collective event (pandemic/health crisis, weather/storm disaster, mass shooting, war [invasion or civil], and more), or as an institutional oppression (racism, sexism, ableism, ageism, homelessness, incarceration, religious persecution, and the list goes on). Trauma manifests in writing in a variety of ways, and knowing what a writer's motivation is for composing and the writer's desire is for sharing can help shape the way one offers feedback to the draft. These are patterns. The only way to know is to ask.

Reading: What Shows Up (or Is Absent) in the Draft?	Responding: Feedback Considerations
Avoidance of details, sensory imagery, or observations, coupled with reliance on narrative drive to push the story forward: telling not showing	The writer needs to feel they are *heard* and in control/in charge of their narrative. Consider what asking for details/evidence might suggest to the writer in the context of their trauma. What would it cost the writer to return to the site of trauma (memories), and would that be retraumatizing for them? How can they feel safe (empowered) while generating the details, descriptions, or imagery that embodies the experience? How does grounding the story in observations (versus generalizations) honor the complexity of the self and the trauma experienced?
Absence of narrative drive coupled with collections or clusters of detail, observation, and sensory imagery: showing but not saying	The writer needs to feel they are *seen* and that the details and imagery they offer are "real" or "relatable" or inhabitable. Consider what asking for narrative might suggest to the writer in the context of their trauma. A narrative offers a shape to the story—shapes have meanings (Dori Laub). Would establishing a storyline force a false sense of causality, congruity, or coherence on the experience that is inauthentic to the writer (supports master narratives versus counterstories)? How might the choice to subvert a narrative or to experiment with a creative narrative form (a more authentic shape) honor the complexity of the self and the trauma experienced?
A reflection (conclusions) that does not align with the narrative told or the details shared: a "canned" conclusion on top of a thoughtfully developed story	The writer needs to feel they are *accepted* and that the story they share makes "sense" and has "value" to their audience. Consider what prying open the reflection/conclusions or introducing uncertainty, impermanence, or exploration might do to their relationship with the story and their sense of authority. What would unpacking cliches, generalizations, or platitudes cost the writer in security? How might the opportunity to lessen the burden of explaining, the weight of reasoning, and the desire to fit the able-bodied, able-minded narrative of "healthy"/healed offer the writer a more authentic truth—an acknowledgment of their own story?

Reading: What Shows Up (or Is Absent) in the Draft?	Responding: Feedback Considerations
The absence of reflection or contemplation and the reliance on narrative drive or sensory imagery to re-create the experience of trauma without context or intent: this has been called unofficially "trauma porn"	The writer needs to feel *empathy*, and they invite the reader deep into their experience and body so they too can viscerally, emotionally, mentally, and spiritually feel what it is like to be them in that moment. The moment they are inviting one into is trauma; if, as Roland Barthes claims, the story is finished in the reader, then this trauma has been passed on and through to the reader. What would suggesting context, intent, reflection, or contemplation cost the writer in aesthetic appeal or creative expression? (See "Part One: Consumption") How might the choice to include the significance of telling the narrative (reflection) or exploring through narrative the complexities (contemplation) create the space for radical compassion and the invitation (would you like to enter) for empathy?
The writing demonstrates little awareness of temporality in the draft. Tenses are unintentionally inconsistent, locked in the past (even when describing), or perpetually in the present (even when reflecting)	The writer needs to feel *safe*, and they monitor how close they and their reader can get to the site of trauma and the pace at which they travel through space and time. Temporality in the context of writing that reveals trauma can indicate if the writer is still living, experiencing, existing in the trauma (be it event or chronic state) or if they perceive that their trauma is in the past (post-trauma) and unlikely to recur. Most writers are somewhere between these extremes. What might it cost the writer to go back in time or back in body to the experience, and what would be the purpose of the mission? Is it for fact finding and honoring truth or is it for exploiting the trauma to achieve artistic expression/aesthetic appeal? How might the choice to modulate between past and present (and even future) help the writer learn more about their relationship to the trauma—their relationship to the story of suffering?

Reading: What Shows Up (or Is Absent) in the Draft?	**Responding: Feedback Considerations**
The writing demonstrates little awareness or intentional choice about point of view/ perspective: it jumps from first to third to second to . . . or it stays firmly planted in first, third, or second, even when shifting between showing, telling, and reflecting	The writer needs to feel *agency*, and they are seeking an authorial and authoritative voice/lens that can support this. Each POV offers different limitations and access points; what would it cost the writer to experiment with these vantage points? How might this play with POV give the writer more access to the relationship they have to the story and their motivation for writing it: blame, shame, guilt, justice, equity, fairness, truth, honor, trust, hope, fear, love, purpose, and more?
The structure of the writing demonstrates little attention to organization, sequence, or shape: (globally) it may appear as a big block of prose or synthetically derived paragraph breaks or lacking cohesion; (regionally) it may appear as incoherent or jumps in logic or artificial use of transitions; or (locally, on the line level) as unintentional fragments, comma splices, dangling modifiers, run-on sentences, etc.	The writer needs to feel *understood*, and yet they reflect how hard it is to organize, make sense of, and share the way that trauma has disrupted their own narrative. What would it cost the writer to experiment with different structures, forms, shapes, and genres until they find the one that fits? How might this play seem on the surface to "trivialize" the trauma (make an exercise of it)? How must intention and truth be centered in order to make this risk meaningful? What might the author gain by attending to structure?
The writer has come to every class and yet still provides no draft at all	The writer needs to feel *support*. Right place. Right time. Are they ready to write this? What might complicate their desire to write it and their motivation to complete it?

Summative Assessment: Grading and Rubrics

One of the most common questions we hear from high school teachers and university faculty is, "How do we grade personal writing?" How can we assign numbers to a story about a parent who was murdered or someone who was in a tragic car accident? If the grade is not an "A," does this mean that their experience is less valuable than another? Some high school teachers have admitted to avoiding personal writing completely so that they do not have to worry about grading papers that are deeply personal. Turley and Gallagher (2008) offer a comprehensive evaluation of the "to rubric-or-not-to-rubric debate." In conclusion, they assert: "While the language of the rubric represents a consensus of the values of this community of writers, it is also a launching point for conversation: a place to start, and never a place to end" (92). Assessing student writing that reveals trauma further complicates the conversation on the deployment of rubrics.

As reflected in earlier chapters on assignment design, revision coaching, and peer workshopping, we are advocates of a draft-driven approach to composition. By assuming this position, we note that formative assessment of the rough draft, driven by "margin" feedback, holistic reflection, and triage endnotes that align with the rubric replicates the writing as a conversation model endorsed by composition/rhetoric scholars such as Barbara Wallraf and Mike Palmquist. What, then, do we do when the final draft—the product—is submitted? Can a piece of student writing that reveals the experience of trauma be graded? Should it?

In the article "In the Absence of Grades: Dissonance and Desire in Course-Contract Classrooms," Inman and Powell (2018) examine the role of grades as signifiers/markers/symbols for achievement, progress, belonging, and institutional values, and because they serve as such, they become part of the identity of students: "A" student, "C" student, etc. Inman and Powell analyze the results of a study on course contracts in composition classrooms and offer two interpretations for the data. The quantitative survey data indicated that students were satisfied with the course contract that emphasized labor and expectations over grades/marks; however, the qualitative data indicated that students "desired" the grade—felt lost, displaced, uneasy without it. Inman and Powell argue that the decolonization of the academy by subverting grades and positioning students as writers instead of students puts an undue burden on the students by ignoring or dismissing the affective attachment to/of grades.

We pose that by using a rubric that accurately and authentically rewards risk, play, and experimentation, we are creating a space where compositions that explore counternarratives, traumatic experiences, or positionality stories can be equitably assessed. Because rubrics "reflect the values" of a community, including this dimension in the creation of the tool reinforces that risk, play, and experimentation is rewarded *and* how the stories that subvert dominant ideologies, the lived experiences that counter mainstream stories, and the people bravely sharing these compositions are valued. Assigning a grade to the piece of writing further reinforces that this writing belongs here, and this writer belongs here. Using the rubric to assign the grade also helps to promote that the *writing* is being graded, not the trauma and certainly not the writer. Managing the expectations of the student submitting the work starts in the first feedback encounter: what do they hope to feel, know, see, and/or receive when this paper is submitted versus returned? What was their intention for the investigation and motivation of the rhetorical choices in the composition?

Just as we asked what the instructor's intention was behind the messy-draft feedback, we return here to the larger questions: 1) what do I hope the students will learn through this assignment?; 2) what do I see as the role of this assignment in my course design?; 3) what do I see as the purpose of this course?; and 4) how does this course fit in with my philosophy of teaching? If schools and instructors are inspired to adopt curricula that are equitable, inclusive, and diverse, then they must let this shift in paradigm inform grade-contracts, pedagogy, and assessment. Using old tools to assess new mindsets will be misleading; using new tools to assess old mindsets will be telling.

As noted in the early work of composition legends Peter Elbow and David Bartholomae (1995), as the difficulty of the content increases, so, too, do the structural and grammatical errors in the text. Likewise, when students are exploring familiar or comfortable content, fewer structural and grammatical errors exist in the text. Trauma further complicates these claims, because in the "errors" and/or diversions from the "assignment," valuable information about the relationship the writer has to the story they are telling (and thus, the trauma they are negotiating on the page) emerges. This messy-draft moment can offer opportunities for creatively, critically, and contemplatively approaching the text; they are the markers for writerly choices. Choice here, in the context of trauma writing, is not just a symbolic gesture but rather a realized act of empowerment. How can the writer reclaim some of the power they have lost when experiencing trauma by developing agency in the construction of their story?

On the table that appears on the following page, we include the rubric we developed and used.

EXPLORATORY (+5 PTS)	CRITERIA	EXEMPLARY (90–95%)
Takes a risk in content. Writes the edge.	CONTROLLING IDEA	Clearly defined Highly engaging/ immediately captures reader's attention
Attempts experimental form/structure to create a space for the text.	ORGANIZATION/ STRUCTURE	Consistently logical structure in paragraphs and essay as a whole
Achieves a multifocal awareness: Reader can see the waves (details) in the ocean (significance) and the ocean in each wave. Intentional. Contemplative.	EVIDENCE OF DEEP PROCESSING/REFLECTION	Strongly creative or imaginative in approach Strong evidence of thinking about the controlling idea and identifying its significance
Practices sensory imagery, literary devices, and syntax to manifest the intention of the piece.	EFFECTIVE SELECTION USE OF DETAIL	Well-developed and relevant details consistently used to support controlling idea
	MECHANICS/ CORRECTNESS	No or very few errors in grammar, punctuation, word usage.

This is why we present here a rubric that privileges "Exploratory" over "Exemplary." The original rubric was developed by faculty at Bryant University in the launch of their Gateway Program. The Writing Workshop Community of Practice used the AACU

(Association of American Colleges and Universities) Value Rubrics for Reflective Writing and Critical Analysis to establish their criteria for measure. We added on to this rubric the column "Exploratory" to emphasize the significance of writing not just as a process but also the value of processing through the act of writing. Note that "trauma" is not "rewarded" or "measured" or even mentioned in the rubric, but risk, wager, play, and experimentation are framed. A writer could take a risk in form that fails and still be rewarded for the risk, whereas if they took the risk in form without this category they would lose significant points on the paper if it did not "succeed." There would be no incentive to try something that might fail—to reach. If a student decides to "play it safe" in content, form, and craft, then they can still earn an "A" (95 percent), but they cannot exceed that ceiling without venturing outside of their comfort zone. This is where collecting process letters with final drafts becomes useful because the students can self-report what they wagered and how/why.

Chapter 7: Questions for Reflection

1. How do we encourage our peers to implement similar rubrics when faculty have been shown to avoid inviting difficult conversations into the classroom?
2. How can this type of rubric be used on different types of assignments across grade levels and disciplines?
3. Revisit a personal essay you had difficulty grading or had difficulty writing. In rereading, what do you notice about the piece? Can you identify the places of resistance or sprawl or block or reach? Which areas of your rubric do they complicate? How would you respond for formative assessment? Summative?
4. The chart on reading and responding in this chapter is the synthesis of years of observations recorded in teaching journals, conversations with colleagues, and end-of-semester reflections on praxis. What types of tools do you use to record and reflect? What patterns do you notice in your students' writing? In your own?

8

Reading Trauma in Our Students' Writing—Too Many Taylors

In this section, Kristen provides an example of identifying and responding to the patterns listed in Chapter 7 by reading the draft, approaching the writer, generating feedback, and offering writerly choices to empower the student. This is intended as a space to explore the raw process and expose both the difficulties and the value of working with a trauma-sensitive pedagogy.

> I'm not sure it is possible to articulate grief through language. You can say, I was so sad I thought my bones would collapse. I thought I would die. But language always falls short of the body when it comes to the intensity of corporeal experience. The best we can do is bring language in relationship to corporeal experience-bring words close to the body-as close as possible. Close enough to shatter them. Or close enough to knock a body out. To bring language close to the intensity of experiences like love or death or grief or pain is to push on the affect of language. Its sounds and grunts and ecstatic noises. The ritual sense of language. Or the cry.
>
> — Lidia Yuknavitch, *The Chronology of Water*

> Your life doesn't happen in any kind of order. Events don't have cause and effect relationships the way you wish they did. It's all a series of fragments and repetitions and pattern formations. Language and water have this in common.
>
> — Lidia Yuknavitch, *The Chronology of Water*

Trigger Warning

#METOO: Too Many Taylors (Trigger warning: This section discusses sexual assault as it is presented in personal essays.)

According to the Office on Women's Health in the US Department of Health and Human Services, one in five college women have experienced sexual assault. Some of these are students who enroll in our courses, acquire the assigned reading (chapter 5), engage with their peers (chapter 4), and hand in written drafts (chapter 7). In this chapter, I name these students the Taylors to both protect the identities of my students who have shared their work in class as well as to show the diversity in response to trauma. Sadly, I have read the messy drafts of too many Taylors, knowing that for each student who writes about their trauma, there are so many more who do not. And for each Taylor (identifying as "female"), there is also a Tayler (identifying as nonbinary, male, or transgender). The stories of the Taylors arrive on the page in varying degrees of "closeness" to the event. While "closeness" can be read as recency, this is actually not a predictable or useful way of framing it in the context of trauma. "Closeness" in trauma relates more to how "close" the writer is able and willing to get to the memory of the event—the fault line—without retraumatizing themselves. How much emotional, intellectual, and spiritual discomfort (suffering) can the body sit with and how much emotional, intellectual, and spiritual discomfort will the self permit? In experimental prose, this is referred to as writing at the edge. The edge is a place to be respected; the writer does not need to hurl themselves off the cliff to write (and potentially heal from) their trauma (Lascelles, 2018, pp.133–138). I will share here amalgamations of the Taylors—the patterns—so as not to reveal any identifying characteristics of the stories shared or the students who shared them. I will set up here how the messy drafts arrive so that we can explore what type of feedback will be useful when meeting the writer and the writing where they are on the page.

For the narrative/personal essay assignment, I always dedicate a class period to in-class timed freewriting/automatic writing. I don't collect it. I don't walk around and look to see that they're doing it. I sit with them and write—the whole time—and I hold the space. This generative period is an open time to explore the different topics and notice what thoughts, sensations, and feelings emerge as they try on the prompts. After the freewrite, I ask the students to process the experience: highlight the line where you started to get a flood of writing (where words were available to you); tag the themes that those sections explore (#IdentityCrisis; #MyParentsArePeople; #BrokenHeart; #SheGetsMe); highlight the spot where you got stuck (where the words were not available to you); tag the themes that section might have said or note the thoughts, feelings, sensations you experienced when you felt stuck. (See chapter 6 for theory on and examples of assignment design.) Note that *none* of the assignments directly ask that students write about their trauma. Also, as previously reported, students arrive in their bodies in their seats with trauma; writing makes the invisible visible. The Taylors are already there, here, sitting—sometimes invisible, mostly unheard.

Because the class is a workshop and students will be asked to share their work, I have them turn to their neighbor and list off the #tags and ask: what would be most meaningful for you to hear a piece about right now? And then ask back: what would be most meaningful for you to write about right now? Sometimes there is a gap, but in this gap, the student makes their first writerly choice for this paper. The students exit still tossing ideas around as they enter draft two of the messy-draft club. The Taylors most often stay after to talk.

The first Taylor I will discuss is the Taylor whose body-mind-spirit needs justice. There is a truth that needs to be told. This Taylor is both the easiest to work with and the most difficult because they have already made up their mind (but not necessarily their body and spirit) that they are "over it" and have "overcome it." How will I know this Taylor has arrived? Their draft will be driven by narrative but lacking detail, in chronological order as a timeline of events, written in the past tense, and ending with a reflection on the key points that they "learned" and/or "overcame" from the event. There may be platitudes or generalizations but seldom questions. The case will be closed. If Taylor was writing about anything other than trauma, it would be a logical set of criteria for developing a topic, but Taylor has chosen to write about sexual assault on their own person. Remembering the exact order of the night demonstrates that they have walked (and often been walked) through it to piece together and look for cause—to find a reason for why or how this could have happened—a chain to link or a rope to follow out of here. There is a reclaiming of power in the ordering of the night but only if all the "facts" are also truths, and only if all the facts and truths are sequenced in service of shedding shame, revealing what happened (versus might have, could have, should have, ought to have happened), and reconciling the experience of the body, the mind, and the spirit.

The language of a "fact-finding mission" is used in Title IX investigations to reflect this process. When Taylor starts to edit out, disregard, or divorce themself from any facts that don't add up to the rational or concrete story, their whole truth is not spoken. When a person's body is violated by another body, there are many facts that do not line up: why me and if-then (the self) are deeply unsettled by this seismic disruption. As we have seen in chapter 3 and will revisit in chapter 9, Bessel van der Kolk and Peter Levine remind us that the body "keeps the score." Each time Taylor crystallizes the memory to serve the story (not their body or spirit), scar tissue—adhesions—build and thus limit access.

Writing in the past tense allows them to create distance from the event and thus to claim safety and knowledge. In a study on the autoethnographic voice in academic writing, Sophie Tamas (2009) examines this space:

> We are talking about being broken and undone. But our voices as we speak do not sound broken. We sound okay, in fact. What we're talking about sure is awful but our narrative voice seems to have it all worked out. We know what happened and we can talk about it in full sentences that make sense. We can tell others, even strangers, the truth about our experiences. We seem to have found a way to perform an internal god trick, standing outside and above ourselves in order to speak dispassionately about passion. That's how we turn trauma into knowledge (par. 10).

Knowledge is not the same thing as wisdom. Is it the role of academics to produce knowledge and/or wisdom? Is it the place of the instructor to ask for one or the other? If trauma disrupts time, then how does the twelve-year-old, the eighteen-year-old, the twenty-five-year-old, the sixty-eight-year-old body negotiate words like "maturity" and "sophistication" and "wisdom"? How does trauma effect not age but aging? How does the body of work reveal the writer's relationship to the event in the context of time and through the creation of space: tense, POV, and details?

Tamas (2009) demonstrates the danger of asking writers in academia to privilege direct, linear, "clean" texts when researching or writing trauma: "Erasing our inner voices does the same thing. It is a lie of omission. We participate in this lie because we like to see ourselves as coherent, knowledgeable and safe, just like our scholarly voices sound. . . . What breaks my heart also breaks my tongue" (par. 11). Whether our students are writing academic papers (as Tamas describes here) or creative nonfiction memoirs and personal narratives, it feels important to stress that just because a draft is "clean" doesn't mean the writer is "healed." In chapter 5, we explored how trauma is captured in literature—crafted and beautiful in all its visceral horror, utterly sublime. If our students understand trauma narratives from the lens of studying literature and studying in academia, then they, too, will assume that their stories must soundly mark the page: the pen a scalpel, exacting and true.

Taylors' messy drafts are not presenting as messy at all. The tight conclusions leave no room for question, no invitation to revisit, and often pull the bookends or closed-circle structure. They share the knowledge they have gained, the advice or warnings they offer, and at best the "you are not alone" (#metoo) assertion and at worst the "you will get over (beat, win, overcome, conquer) it, too." Perhaps this sounds deeply critical of me to say about the Taylors; don't I want them to be done with the suffering and pain? To put it behind them? I do. I really do. But I also know that using the language of the perpetrator—beat, slay, slam, win, defeat, overtake, conquer, conquest, nail, knock, overcome—to describe the experience of negotiating physical bodily trauma (assault) is flipping a binary. In an interview with Krista Tippett in the podcast *OnBeing*, Ocean Vuong, embodied poet, novelist, and writing instructor, shared:

> We pride ourselves, as a country that's very technologically advanced—we have strong, good sciences; good schools; very advanced weaponry, for sure—but I think we're still very primitive in the way we use language and speak, particularly in how we celebrate ourselves. "You're killing it." . . . We have to ask — I'm not saying it's wrong, per se; I use it too, being a product of this country. But one has to wonder, what is it about a culture that can only value itself through the lexicon of death? . . . What happens to our imagination, when we can only celebrate ourselves through our very vanishing? (18:18–19:23).

Does Taylor reclaim power or empower or surrender power in the language and image of the perpetrator? This depends on the Taylor. This is where feedback gets tricky, very tricky, indeed. Are the Taylors rewarded in/by the justice system for remembering the order of events, and does this contribute to rationalization versus reconciliation?

Because Taylors' messy drafts are not messy at all, any feedback may be rejected completely or misinterpreted as an attempt to undermine, devalue, or question what happened to them, why it happened to them, and in fact, "Her/Him/They"—the very Taylor they are hoping to preserve and protect. If I suspect that Taylor is not being honest with the body, mind, or spirit, not about what happened—the trauma—but of how it injured and continues to injure them, then they are still suffering beneath the scar. This may or may not be the right time in Taylor's life to unpack, to set up deep tissue massages that feel like bruises for days after. Readiness is essential. But they did bring it up. Now. Here. And, yet. And, so, if I say nothing, Taylor keeps the knowledge, but if we do talk, Taylor might open themselves to their own wisdom—the integration of their truth into their body, heart, and mind.

After I holistically read Taylor's draft (no pen is even in my hand/no document has been downloaded and resaved in Word), I refrain from marking the text. My feedback begins with the email on the following page.

Dear Taylor,

Thank you for sharing your experience. It is courageous of you to make yourself vulnerable on the page as you reexamine an event in your life that has caused (and may still cause) you deep suffering. How do you feel now after you have written and submitted this draft?

Do I have your permission to provide feedback on this draft? Would you prefer to first meet in person to review together the draft (a dialogue) or for me to generate notes in the margin of the page that create a conversation in the draft (after which, of course, we can meet to discuss, if you wish)?

Best,

KPW

First, I acknowledge that trauma in the form of a violation against one's body exists and that deciding to share this shows courage (agency). Can't I assume that the Taylors want feedback on the draft because they handed it in to me; won't this extra step slow everything down; will the Taylors feel called out for taking a risk? Admittedly, this took many failed attempts at understanding the Taylors, but no, I should not assume that I have any more permission to write on this text than those who assumed that what the Taylors were wearing, thinking, doing, saying, drinking, or smiling at was permission enough to violate them. Asking consent establishes respect while also acknowledging the body of work: I see you; I hear you; I am here with you. May we proceed together? Asking Taylor to choose the mode and space in which we start this writing conversation encourages them to consider how and if they are open to feedback and what type. Using the messy-draft stage to determine why or how this traumatic memory is being recalled now in the context of the writing prompts (note, again, that none of the prompts ask a student to expose trauma) provides information to the writer and the instructor about one's relationship to the material.

I reflect back to the writer the themes that are emerging in this draft (#themes) and offer the potential subtexts this piece of writing can invoke. Then I ask which of these themes do they also hear or recognize in their piece; which ones have I missed that they caught? This approach indicates what is available in this draft to be developed and provides the writer with an opportunity to say "yes, let's continue" or "no, that's not it." Using the feedback and revision stages to determine the motivation for continuing to shape and craft the composition and/or for facilitating the setting of an intention with the writer—what I hope to cultivate in this piece—helps to manage the expectations of the writing, the writer, and the instructor. This is the place where the writing instructor can remind the writer that while writing is therapeutic, it is not therapy (Hurley, 2004). I am not a therapist. In what ways does Taylor seek justice? Witness? Truth? Discovery? Empathy? Healing? Expression? Relief? Catharsis? Hope? I want Taylor to know that I can read and listen empathically, but they also need to know that I am not qualified to heal them.

This example helps to clarify the "don't fix the writing" (and "don't fix the writer") mantra in writing center and composition pedagogy. When encountering a draft like Taylor's, one that is driven by narrative but lacking detail—in chronological order as a timeline of events, written in the past tense, and ending with a reflection on the key points that they "learned" and/or "overcame" from the event—here are some recommendations from my research, experience, and own writing practice. While the rubric indicates that the narrative/personal essay requires specific details, narrative drive, and reflective moments, framing how this information is delivered to the Taylors is critical.

In this sample, Taylor is avoiding sensory imagery or vivid detail in favor of narrative drive; they are telling us what it was like instead of showing us what it is like. If I comment "need more evidence or details," I risk Taylor interpreting this as "I don't believe you"; "I don't think this is possible"; "are you sure this is what happened"? The very word "evidence" in the context of assault can be a trigger. I risk shaming Taylor, not addressing the writing, and showing that I have not "heard" what they are telling me in both the absence and presence on the page. I then need to be clear about what my motivation is here: do I want Taylor to reveal all of the visceral details because it will make a more interesting and engaging piece of writing (only serving the text and potentially exploiting Taylor and their trauma)? Do I want Taylor to avoid being retraumatized, so I don't say anything about the absence of the details at all (only serving to "protect" myself and the writer)? Do I want Taylor to reexamine their relationship to the trauma, to embody the experience, and to write toward healing, perhaps, sitting with the scar and acknowledging why and how it formed to protect them? Will drawing the details to the surface offer new conclusions that would serve the writing and the writer but test my ability to hold this space as an instructor? Are Taylor and I committed to seeing this writing project through? Can we both tell each other if we are not ready to do the work it will take to write at the edge? Does the school we are both working in have sufficient resources for supporting the socio-emotional journey Taylor is going to take?

The writing instructor is not a therapist.

So, what can I say instead, or rather, how can I say it instead? (Note that this may happen in person or it may happen in the margins, depending on our contract.) I can appeal to Taylor's authority of their story (the content) by asking them to stretch the language or sentence structure (form). Taylor has found strength and power in "telling" their story. I invite them to play with blending concrete and abstract descriptors and punctuation that vacillates between show and tell (parenthesis and em dashes).

> ***Excerpt from the Taylors:*** *As soon as I sat in the backseat of the car, I knew it was a* ***mistake****. Then we pulled up not to my house but to an unknown house. I felt fear and started to plan an* ***escape****.*

Highlighting a sentence that includes several abstractions, we take one of them and brainstorm five to eight concrete descriptors that define that abstraction; the language is stretched to create room around the memory, an invitation to reenter (see chapter 6 for Apple Exercise on concrete versus abstract language). Then, they select the three that for them best define the concept in that moment; Taylor lets the language snap back against the memory, fitting it like an ankle support or knee brace instead of a Band-Aid.

> ***Excerpt from the Taylors:*** *Fear: stomach dropped, head spun, wobbled on heels, stretched out arms for balance, frantically searched for my phone, noticed hair on the back of my neck rise, remembered how he tried to steady me, recalled his hand hot on the top of my prickling skin . . .*
>
> *As soon as I sat in the backseat of the car, I knew it was a* **mistake***. Then we pulled up not to my house but to an unknown house. I felt* ***fear as my stomach dropped, heels wobbled, hair prickled on the back of my neck, and his hand on my neck felt warm against the goosebumped skin, almost steadying, and then I*** *started to plan an escape.*

As Taylor adds these concrete details to expand on the abstract concept of fear, I encourage them to take stock of what it feels like in the rest of the sentence but also to hear it in their own body, heart, and mind. The Taylors react: "I don't like that I let myself think his hand was 'steadying,' it makes it look like I wanted it, like I didn't know what I was getting into, like I was too out of it to know what really happened, like I felt more than fear, like I am gullible, like I could be persuaded to go along with anything, like I was not clear about not wanting to be there, like . . ." Some Taylors don't say anything at all—anger, sadness, confusion, hurt show themselves in their bodies, emotions that are different from fear. The fear becomes complicated but so does the trauma. So does the story. So are the Taylors.

An alternative suggestion to the concrete/abstract detail approach is to use the punctuation to stretch the memory and rewalk the line. By using parentheses to determine where asides belong (the intimate moments we share with a select few) or em dashes—driving the sentence forward with charge and purpose—the Taylors are forced to stop and disrupt their own story without detracting from its narrative authority but rather by adding layers of complexity to the voice. Having power over the pacing can make revisiting a memory—what we want to speed up and what we are willing to slow down—accessible to the writer.

> *As soon as I sat in the backseat of the car, I knew it was a* ***mistake (I noticed the phone buzzed in my purse, but I couldn't move my fingers to answer it).*** *Then we pulled up not to my house—****with the flower-lined path, my cat sitting in the window, and a light always on waiting for me****—but to an unknown house. I felt* ***fear as my stomach dropped, heels wobbled, hair prickled on the back of my neck, and his hand felt warm against the goosebumped skin, almost steadying, and then I*** *started to plan an* ***escape.***

If a writer is not ready to tap into visceral or somatic elements of the memory, or it is still unavailable, then the punctuation can still help to add complexity to the story (reduction contributes to memory crystallization) and give the writer room to loosen not their conclusions about the events but rather how the events have or could have an effect on their experience of self, body, identity, and wellness.

Writers of trauma who stay exclusively in the past tense and couple this with tight, closed conclusions create a tone of authority, confidence, and triumph, but the coupling (especially in the absence of any visceral details or somatic memory reflection) often creates a mood that is cold or distant. But this is academia; shouldn't we be writing with an objective and dispassionate tone?

Tamas (2009) helps us note the distinction between dispassionate and disembodied. I return to Tamas's words as in my feedback I extend the writer permission to break the "survivor" narrative and create room for exploration:

> It implies that the order of the universe is, in fact, intact, and the traumatized who have lost faith in reason, language, and human decency are mistaken. I do not think realizing that we are utterly lost and broken necessarily causes despair. What breaks us is the impression that everyone else isn't. Clean and reasonable scholarship about messy, unreasonable experiences is an exercise in alienation. (par. 18)

It is important to distinguish that I am not endorsing putting "cracks" in the story to create an unreliable or subjective narrator—that is not advisable—but I am encouraging the stretch of the line so that the writer can see what resonance and discord still exists at the site of the scar. In chapter 5, we noted that Blanche and Amir remain frozen—stuck in their experiences. How does a crack become a site of growth? If, at this point, Taylor says that they are writing this story not as a space for self-reflection and exploration but as a piece of writing to inspire or help others who have been sexually assaulted, we turn back to the rhetorical situation: narrative/personal essay (not argument paper or speech). You don't have to have all the answers in order to heal or to heal others; you only need a willingness to listen to your own truth—to write it even when you can't right it.

I then invite these writers to take a passage, particularly where action occurred ("language in action," action in language), and rewrite it in present tense. Stepping back into the moment is the place where the writer needs the most support.

> *Slipping into the backseat of the Uber, hair snapping with static electricity, I half-snort a laugh, but then the slamming of the door shut locks me into the moment.* ***(My phone buzzes in my purse but my fingers fumble to answer it.)*** *My brain shouts, "This is a mistake." We pull up not to my house—* ***with the flower-lined path, my cat sitting in the window, and a light always on waiting for me*** *—but to an unknown house. Fear:* ***my stomach drops, heels wobble, hair prickles on the back of my neck. and his hand is warm against the goosebumps on my skin; it is almost steadying, so I . . .***

The Taylors were committed to planning an escape right from the moment they first felt fear, but unpacking the complexity of their fear can take away the cause-and-effect logic that had once driven their story. It is important to remind the writer to ground themselves: put your feet on the floor, hands on the table, breathe, I am here now, and I am safe here. The writer has nothing to prove to the reader, to the parent, to the officer, to the friends, to the instructor because they are *not* on trial, they are *not* guilty, they are not responsible, it is not their fault no matter how that "so, I" sentence ends. Chapter 5 discussed the way that possession shows up in Hamlet and Ophelia's love exchange. For the Taylors, the need to own the story is as much about rejecting Ophelia as it is about embodying Hamlet.

This is a place where I invite the Taylors to step back into the past tense, to re-create the distance between themselves and the moment, and to reflect on how they feel right now, writing this. What do they now know in writing back and through the line? How does disrupting the narrative create discomfort but also space—the untethered or floating fear, the flopping or flouncing fear, the sinking or spreading fear? The thumb in the knot ripples the pain until it doesn't. By taking the end-loaded focus of the reflection and distributing it throughout the text in the form of questions, inner thoughts, or embodied remembering, the writer can suture their story without suffocating it. This also avoids the challenge of dismantling platitudes or generalizations in the conclusion: "Everything happens for a reason"; "I had to go through this to see how strong I am"; "Time is the greatest healer"; "You, too, will be fine one day." These flat claims often dilute or silence the more authentic truths discovered not in the "rethinking" about the event but in the writing of the event.

> *Slipping into the backseat of the Uber, hair snapping with static electricity, I half-snort a laugh, but then the slamming of the door shut locks me into the moment.* ***(My phone buzzes in my purse but my fingers fumble to answer it.)*** *My brain shouts, "This is a mistake." We pull up not to my house—* ***with the flower-lined path, my cat sitting in the window, and a light always on waiting for me*** *—but to an unknown house. Fear:* ***my stomach drops, heels wobble, hair prickles on the back of my neck, and his hand is warm against the goosebumps on my skin; it is almost steadying, so I. . . . I stop myself not in the moment but here in the memory of it, to remind myself that what happens next is not my fault.***

or

> *Slipping into the backseat of the Uber, hair snapping with static electricity, I half-snort a laugh, but then the slamming of the door shut locks me into the moment.* ***(My phone buzzes in my purse but my fingers fumble to answer it.)*** *My brain shouts, "This is a mistake." We pull up not to my house—* ***with the flower-lined path, my cat sitting in the window, and a light always on waiting for me*** *—but to an unknown house. Fear:* ***my stomach drops, heels wobble, hair prickles on the back of my neck, and his hand on my neck is warm against the goosebumps on my skin; it is almost steadying, so I. . . . All I had wanted, all I had planned on, was a night of dancing with friends, but I found myself alone. Except for the hand on my neck.***

This is not the only way the Taylors show up on the page, but I started here because many of these conventional strategies for providing feedback can also be applied to the other ways in which trauma shows up in the page: 1) holistic reading and reflective response; 2) asking permission and setting up feedback environments; 3) finding strategies that honor the rubric and the writer/writing; and 4) sharing observations and offering choices.

Here are two more patterns (although there are so many variations out there) that manifest in writing about trauma that violate the body, and a rationale for the types of feedback I offered. The Taylors who choose to write about their sexual trauma but report experiencing a blackout of the event (see chapter 3 for neuroscience of trauma) come to the page with a gap in the narrative that they struggle to fill. The dissociation explored in chapter 5 (Feldman and Frederickson) occurs both in the body and on the page—the Taylors step out. Sometimes these Taylors do not hand in a rough draft. Their writer's block is not just a block in writing; it is a block in accessing the material they have set out to write. This feels like a betrayal of the body to the self and the self to the body—a secret that promises relief if it can only be exorcised. But this is trauma, and there are no guarantees here that reinhabiting the dark moment will bring justice or healing or truth. There is a reason why the body will not give the mind access to the sensation or somatic memory of the experience. Protection is only one of the reasons, but it is a good place to start.

Taylor's final draft was due in two hours, and they sat in front of me with the crumpled up freewrite from class two weeks ago. After going through the previously described exchange of information, motivation, and intention, we sit with the crumpled paper, and I ask if they want to write this story. "I am here, aren't I?" the paper says. Taylor tells their story, the parts they do remember, and I listen. When they get to the moment where they are returning to the last thing they remember before the rape, they stop. The Taylors start: "I don't know why I can't remember; I don't remember feeling anything; not being able to remember feeling it makes me feel like it might not have really happened; maybe I just imagined it happening and then how sick is that; where did I go; I was there, but I wasn't there; it doesn't seem right or real; nothing adds up; it doesn't fit; what can I do with this; if I can't believe it, then nobody else will; I only remember their (eyes, smell, breath, hair), but I don't remember myself." The Taylors are frustrated and angry and sad and ashamed and betrayed. The Taylors are still hurting not just from the event but from also confronting the event, always looking for a new way in.

I ask: where do you go when it is happening? Some of the Taylors stand next to the couch and watch, while others go in their head and create checklists, while some still feel every scream stuck in their head with no way out of their mouth, and there are Taylors who disappear to reappear a few hours or days later. The feedback for these Taylors ranges from 1) inviting the writer to write it as an observer (or in the third person) with an emphasis on radical compassion—*I watched him hurt her and I want to tell her. . . . He raped her, and though no one was there to witness it, it happened*; 2) inviting the writer into the second-person address by choosing a person (themself, the perpetrator, or a bystander) or a part of their own body to write a letter to in order to enlist in the shared memory, not as confession but as confrontation or compassion—*Dear Nailbeds, You know; Dear Girl who Walked Past the Open Door; Dear Rapist . . .* ; 3) inviting the writer to focus on removing this "climactic event" and refocusing the narrative on an alternative moment in the trauma that they can access (reminding them that a single traumatic event can be a four-hundred+ page book, and sometimes one chapter at a time is necessary); 4) inviting the writer to work in another genre like fiction or poetry that gives access to truth even when memory blocks it. All these suggestions take the writer and the assignment out of its traditional context and might receive criticism for "not preparing the student to write academic essays." I challenge this by reminding educators that this is not the only essay the student will ever write, that I am not the only teacher this student will ever have, and that, yes, somebody else can teach them and prepare them for all these future events, but I am the teacher who is here now with this student and this paper that they have chosen to write in my class. Will my rubric still work? Yes. Is this the "easy way out"? No. Will this be fair to other students?

What?!?

Really?!?

The Taylors who are haunted by the memory of the event and / or the memory of their perpetrator may experience an overload of sensory images that evoke visceral responses. They may become physically ill or contracted (blood vessels, muscles) during the excavation of the trauma. While the Taylor with no memory of the event accuses the body of hiding something from the mind, the Taylor with a triggered body response to the memory may accuse the mind of not being able to process, conceptualize, or language the trauma. They can't bear the label, or they name it without feeling and sensing it. This can show up in the rough draft as a giant prose block with no stops or starts—as though they had to get it down all at once before it got them. It can also be a draft that starts, stops, or skips erratically, getting caught up on details and struggling to find a voice, style, or structure. This draft, too, might be crumpled in the bottom of a bag. Or not handed in at all. Many of the same recommendations as were previously listed and alternative assignments can apply here because they moderate the distance between the event and the writer. I cannot stress how important it is for this Taylor to not grab onto a direct, linear narrative. It will only offer temporary comfort—like they have finally figured it out and can put the haunts to rest—but the body will resist the false container. The body will resist being forced to fit. Taylor needs to find an authentic way to embody the writing, to communicate to their own body: I see you, I hear you, and I am with you.

Whether the Taylors have a need for control (Hamlet), dissociate self from body (Willy, Hester, Blanche, and Sethe), or remain frozen in trauma (Blanche, Ophelia, Marlow, and Amir), their stories and their bodies will arrive on the page before us as instructors of English. The same close reading that we practice (see chapter 5 and chapter 10) when we offer texts featuring traumatized characters should be applied to the reading of our students' work. If we want to dignify their trauma (chapter 2) and demonstrate respect through critical and reciprocal witnessing (chapter 6), then it is our responsibility to include trauma literacy in the classroom and trauma-sensitive pedagogy in our assignment designs, feedback, and grading. Sharing readings with our students that demonstrate diverse voices, forms, and approaches to writing fills their toolbox with resources and extends the message that it is okay to reach, fail, rupture, resist, transform, and disrupt narrative structures, and, thus, narrative scripts—the codes that reinforce norms (see chapter 9). Trauma is messy. There is never a big enough closet to stuff it in.

Before I close this section, I breathe with the Taylors: you are seen, you are heard, we are with you.

Chapter 8: Questions for Reflection

1. Does the school in which you work have the resources to support both the Taylors and the teachers of Taylors? What does your school's mental health and wellness program cover? Who does it cover? Have you ever referred a student?
2. Explore the way communication and feedback is exchanged in your classroom. How and from whom do students receive information, expectations, and feedback? How would you facilitate peer workshops and sharing when one of your students reveals they are writing about trauma?
3. In chapter 5, we discussed how our favorite literary characters arrive with their trauma in language that is beautiful and sublime. What does this communicate to students about trauma? About the way to write trauma? About those who have been traumatized? How do you hold the space for messy drafts and unprocessed trauma?
4. Has a Taylor ever shown up in your classroom? How did you know? How did you approach the feedback process? What has worked for you in the past? What edges exist? How do you create boundaries in the relationship and a container on the page to keep both you and the student safe? If you could write a letter to one of your Taylors, what would you say?

III

Embodiment

9

Trauma, Memory, and Narrative

The desire to grasp, to make meaning, to find purpose has been driving pencils to pages since before there were pencils and pages. Storytelling engages the mind, body, and spirit in ways that are deeply satisfying. Broken things become whole, holes become portals, and doors are replaced by windows: the writer shapes the line on which they are walking. Trauma (and being triggered) unsettles not just our story but our relationship to our story. Incidentally, so does meditation. In this chapter, the neuroscience of meditation is coupled with the cognitive science of memory to explore how constructs like language can disrupt or perpetuate habitual thinking. Trauma in this lens can be framed as a growth site. Kristen shares insight meditation and contemplative writing practices to situate vulnerability, uncertainty, and humility as strengths that can build a classroom culture of radical compassion.

> At this point, we are in a very powerful spot: being in the present, we can reshape the whole future. Therefore, shouldn't we be more careful, shouldn't we be more awake in what we are doing this very moment?
>
> —Chogyam Trungpa Rinpoche, *True Perception*

Our phones ping—round after round of notifications—calling out for a precious resource: our attention. When the headlines for traumatic events lap and overlap, it becomes hard to know where to answer the collective wakeup call. Jon Kabat-Zinn, mindfulness leader and molecular biologist, points not to the phone booth or the newsroom or even the cushion but rather to the body. It is time to wake up to ourselves and our world—to come to our senses—through our[cell]ves (Kabat-Zinn,

2005). Inviting mindfulness into the classroom is not just having something to do (a practice) but also inviting an attitude—something to be, together—into the space: Non-Judging, Acceptance, Patience, Beginner's Mind, Trust, Non-Striving, Letting Go, Gratitude, and Generosity (Kabat-Zinn, 1990).

We have already noticed that as we open the door to personal narrative and creative nonfiction—holding the space for examining the human experience and the self—papers filled with the mess of living come shuffling through. It is not surprising that organizations like the Association for Contemplative Mind in Higher Education have responded to the need for trauma-sensitive pedagogy with a series of talks and trainings on how to embody the curriculum to create equitable, mindful, and compassionate learning communities. However, just as trauma-informed pedagogy has been co-opted by the professional development checklist, so, too, has McMindfulness.

To counter this trend of oversimplification, we offer this chapter rooted in the philosophy, science, and art of mindfulness to demonstrate what, why, and how inviting mindfulness into the classroom means to the bodies, minds, and hearts of students and instructors. We tailor this chapter to the English classroom (comp / lit / creative writing / etc.), focusing not on the health benefits of meditation (although there are many!) but instead on the improvements in metacognition, meta-reflection, self-awareness, mindful inquiry, creativity, and receptivity (the very same capacities diminished by unaddressed trauma).

Walking and Waking: All the Selves and Cells

"I never knew how angry I was until I started meditating." They stop—a few snorts, some knitted brows—they are looking me over and waiting. I wear bright-colored scarves, laugh at inappropriate times, smile way too much, and give extensions way too easily (I'm a bit of a softy). It doesn't add up: Professor Wedlock is *nice.* I can see that some of the students are becoming uncomfortable, so I tell the story—reconcile the self and the thoughts and the feelings and the noticing—to provide a container for my sentence, a space to unsettle, to loosen the dirt.

I had just moved to Boulder, Colorado, from New Jersey (climate and culture shock) to start my MFA in writing and poetics at the Jack Kerouac School at Naropa University. Naropa was founded by Chogyam Trungpa Rinpoche, a leader in bringing Tibetan

Buddhism to the West, as well as Anne Waldman and Allen Ginsberg, poet-activists. Each day began with meditation, so I grabbed a cushion on the windowless side of the room (because I have a habit of daydreaming when I see trees swaying); *I was serious; this was serious; everyone here had to know I was serious; I needed everyone here to know Kristen was serious.* It was week three—just when I had started to feel comfortable with sitting meditation (as in, I could return my wandering focus back to my breath, stop internally shouting *look at me I am doing it*, and I only had pins and needles in my right foot, not both)—when the instructor cued us for walking meditation. Attraction: *I like walking; the toe-ball-heel and balancing weight will be just like ballroom—foxtrot; movement, yes, something I can do.*

In less than a lap around the room, sweat runs down my spine faster than the dry Colorado air can wick it away; my breath catches high in my chest, drawing my shoulders to my ears, throwing off my balance; my heart pounds so hard that each pulse registers in my throat and fingertips; and my jaw tightens so that my teeth trap my tongue. Aversion: *Get me out of here; NOW; I am going to puke on the floor; I am suffocating; I am dying; I can't do this; I was a dancer, why can't I fucking walk?!; everyone else is fine; I am NOT fine.* The more I "try" to escape the sensation or dismiss the thoughts, the louder they grow. My body screams: *Don't shut me down*; my mind demands: *Don't turn me off*. Of what was I so afraid? What happened next shook me awake.

The shape of the walker in front of me became clear—the shirt draping in loose cool folds of fabric from the narrow frame—she was barely moving, as if there was all the time in the world, and no one was trying to get anywhere, and I did not exist behind her—the next heel strike a surge of energy ran full circuit from the right side to the left, and as the left foot lifted from the floor, a kick was forming at the knee: *How dare you take up so much space, disregard the pace of the room, waste all of our time.* "I"—thoughts in the moment, wanted to kick this shape, this obstacle, this person in the back of the knees.

Slamming the foot down before making contact with her, the energy boils up from the ground to the belly and breaks through the tightened chest, arms pushing through the air: *How dare you act like I don't exist.* The mouth breather behind me is pouring hot air on the backs of my ears; I imagine his toenails scraping my heel bones: *How dare you pin me; how dare you make me feel small and trapped and stuck and aware of the sweat on my back.* "I" breathes into the widest part of my lungs—the back—my ribcage splays my shoulder blades: *Back off.* "I" am angry. Angry feels different then afraid.

"Witness thoughts, sensations, feelings as they arise, acknowledge them, label them, then return to the breath, to the foot on the floor, to the space between breaths, to the space between footfalls," a voice interjects.

Anger. "I" felt angry, and I really "felt" it—as in, sensed it moving through the body, firing in the brain, and in this movement, it discharged. It didn't erupt onto the person in front of me, but it didn't lodge in my body either. I kept walking not because I was afraid to step out of line and not be the "good listener"—I was out of fear and into something else that felt more powerful, something that made my ears ring with a heartbeat that was mine and alive and sound. "I" finally let myself feel what "me" had resisted for so long. "Me" was not ANGRY, WOMAN; "me" was NICE, GOOD, LITTLE, GIRL—or at least Kristen worked very hard to maintain this narrative (peppered, of course, with a few rebellious moments). The things that had to be done (aka suffering) to hold onto the story of "me" were reactive, habitual, and exhausting.

I tell this story (as I walk around the room weaving in and out of desks) of Professor Wedlock wanting to kick everyone in the back of the knees—feeling all her feelings, thinking all her thoughts, breathing all her breaths—and disrupting all the myths of mindfulness *(you will be blissed out, meditation feels so good, you can just relax for a bit, take a break from your life)* and Western ideas about identity (I think, therefore I am; mind over matter; I am what I do). I offer my experience as both an invitation to be open to whatever arises and in my role as instructor, permission to experience it here, now, together, on purpose, and without judgment.

Sometimes, not always, seldom really, I model unpacking the cells of anger (emotion) stored in my body (which includes the brain) and how mindfulness—through awareness and attention—wakes them up; how language tries to extract these somatic memories; and how narrative seeks to shape and share them. *Breath caught in chest:* wanting who/what you can't (read: shouldn't) have and sternum pinned, splayed like a butterfly to a page with a single hand. *Pulse caught in throat:* a sleeve of Oreos pressing down shame and his hand locked around my throat. *Jaw tightens, teeth trap tongue:* sugar dissolves as panic sets in, "what have you done?" *and* keep him out of mouth, out of in, out of "me"/me. *Fingertips throbbing:* a trigger on the last cookie purging in bliss and feeling for the folded bills in my pocket.

On that day it wasn't fear but rather anger that called my attention to these embodied memories of violence: the kind I had received from other people and the kind I had inflicted on my body. Anger cut through them both in a way that shame and fear could not. That which threatened the narratives of GOOD and LITTLE and GIRL refused to be stuffed back down as I walked between these two fellow meditators, angry and awake.

But then I take my class, and we travel down to the English Garden on campus (our own Zen labyrinth), line up, take the cues for mindful walking, and begin.

"No pushing," I remind. "Self or other."

Mindfulness: Attentional Focus, Emotional and Cognitive Regulation

> "Mindfulness is the awareness that arises from paying attention, on purpose, in the present moment and nonjudgmentally."
>
> —Jon Kabat-Zinn

It is important to make the distinction here between mindfulness and meditation (even if it is only at the semantic level), mostly because "mindfulness" is a universal quality that exists outside of religious and spiritual contexts, whereas meditation, even when taught from a secular frame, is rooted in religious and spiritual teachings and practices. Mindfulness describes being present—experiencing the moment—through attentional awareness. Meditation refers to the practice of attention and awareness. While mindfulness can be experienced during meditation and meditative awareness can cultivate mindfulness, the terms are not interchangeable. If we are bringing mindfulness or meditation into the English classroom, then we risk proselytizing (by endorsing a specific practice) and appropriating (by ignoring the cultural significance). How much of the history, philosophy, and culture that informs when and why sacred texts with meditation instruction were composed needs to be shared with students?

I began my own meditation practice studying Soma Yoga and Embodied Meditation with Bobbie Ellis under a therapeutic/healing lens (to understand my stress and trauma). I continued while a graduate student at Naropa University (applying a dharma/Shambhala arts frame) and during a professional development certificate in contemplative pedagogy at Brown University with Harold Roth, Willoughby Britton, Catherine Kerr, and Jared Lihtal. Brown University introduced me to Jon Kabat-Zinn's Mindfulness Based Stress Reduction (MBSR) program, which offers a secular approach to meditation by situating it in the universality of mindfulness. Kabat-Zinn's MBSR eight-week program was designed for clinical practice in hospital settings and has been adopted by most research studies as the protocol for investigating the effects of mindfulness interventions and meditation practices. In the next section, I offer a literature review of the neuroscience of mindfulness that most directly aligns with the goals and objectives of the English classroom. All the studies analyzed use the MBSR program as part of their methodology. In chapter 6, the embodied writing activities and mindfulness exercises we offered engage this work to create a trauma-sensitive classroom and a trauma literacy course adoptable in public education. We are not endorsing cultural appropriation *or* a hodge-podge dilution of teachings, but rather we are offering a distillation—a tincture.

A significant quality of both meditation and mindfulness is attention. Attention (and attending to attention) forges the connection between writing practice and trauma literacy: on what and whom will we focus and why? The outcomes of using mindfulness practices in the English classroom mirror many of the benefits of reading literature described in chapter 5, including aesthetic engagement, catharsis, empathetic imagination, and critical thinking: "Active attention is the door through which we step out of a life of reaction and habituation and into a life of presence. The energy of active attention penetrates patterns, disrupts their operation, and eventually dismantles them" (McLeod, 2002, p.52). Both trauma and meditation disrupt the stories and scripts we have been conditioned to maintain, which is why as a literature consumed or a narrative produced, they can create the conditions for awakening.

McLeod (2002) described the difference between active attention and passive attention by using the example of a flower. When the flower is resting in our hands, and we focus our attention on the qualities of the flower in the present moment—use our senses to observe and catalog the object—then we are in active attention. When beholding the flower stirs a memory of flowers (or a flower), and we label it "thinking, memory" and then return to this flower, here and now, we are still in active attention. If we follow the memory down the lane—honeysuckle, backyard baseball, broken glasses, perfect pitch, freedom, joy, Sam—and get lost along the way, then we are in passive attention of the flower. We can't be present with the flower *and* present with the cognitive or emotional narrative of the flower at the same time. Our minds are in active attention (experience focused) or passive attention (narrative focused). Consider the implications of this in a reading or writing practice. How might cultivating an observational attention be useful for researchers and writers (aka our students)? In the context of trauma, returning to the present—reminding oneself that I am here, here I am—can be grounding.

Neuroscience of Mindfulness

Body like a mountain
Breath like the wind
Mind like the sky
—Ancient Tibetan Buddhist meditation cue, shared with me by dharma
Poet Reed Bye

While evidence-based research in the science of mindfulness focuses on the well-documented health benefits of meditation practices, this chapter focuses on the regions of the brain and neural mechanisms that are most affected by meditation and that correlate with multiple intelligences—intellectual and socio-emotional intelligence—that can be appreciated in the classroom: "learning and memory processes, emotion regulation, self-referential processing, and perspective taking" (Hölzel et al., 2011).

In part one of this book, we establish that most people (ninety percent) will have experienced trauma in their lives, that experiencing trauma rewires the brain, and yet when encountering literature that includes trauma, most students will not be triggered to the point of retraumatization. What accounts for the difference? Why are some students more resilient than others, and what can we as educators do to develop resilience to adversity? And what are the limitations of focusing on individual resilience in the context of trauma (as opposed to addressing the systems and institutions that perpetuate the conditions for chronic trauma, exploitation, and inequity)?

Studying the relationship between neuroplasticity—the brain's ability to adapt to its environment structurally and functionally—and resilience, neuroscientists, psychologists, and social workers are collaborating to understand the neural mechanisms present when this trait manifests (Hunter et al., 2018). Measuring gray matter activation in the brain before, during, and after mindfulness interventions has become a reliable method in this research. Meditation has been shown to change the prefrontal cortex (Lazar, 2005), default mode network (Judson, 2011), insula cortex (Sharp et al., 2018), anterior cingulate cortex (Hölzel et al., 2017), brain stem (Singleton et al., 2014), thalamus (Zeidan et al., 2012), amygdala (Taren et al., 2015), hippocampus (Hölzel et al., 2011), temporoparietal junction (Hölzel et al., 2011), and cerebral cortex (Luders et al., 2012). Educators who use mindfulness to embody their curricula can contribute to and benefit from this exchange.

Hölzel et al. (2011) focused specifically on the gray matter activation in the hippocampus—important for learning, memory, and emotional processing—and the insula cortex—significant in a sense of interoception. It is important to note that during major depression (Sheline, 2000) and post-traumatic stress disorder (Kasai et al., 2008), the size of the hippocampus is reduced (Hölzel et al,. 2011, 7). Thus, students experiencing post-traumatic injury are operating with a diminished hippocampus; memory, learning, and emotional processing is taxed under the stress of trauma. Hölzel et al. (2011) found that meditators enrolled in the MBSR program demonstrated more gray matter activation than nonmeditators in the hippocampus: here, neuroplasticity is hard at work to build better lines of connectivity. If creating equitable classrooms is at the heart of what we hope to achieve, then providing mindfulness interventions to all our students (those with and without post-traumatic injury) grounds this commitment in practice.

While Hölzel et al. did not find significant improvement in the insula cortex (participants in both the experimental and control groups responded similarly to cues for interoceptive awareness), they did discover increased gray matter activation in the temporoparietal junction (TPJ). Building on the claims of Blanke et al. (2005), Arzy et al. (2006), Van Overwalle (2009), Shapiro et al. (2006), and Carmody (2009) that the TPJ is important in experiencing the self and the body as well as the selves and bodies of others, Hölzel et al. determined that increased gray matter activation in the TPJ after MBSR training could support the value of mindfulness in cultivating an embodied and compassionate self. Blanke et al. (2005) noted that impairment of the TPJ often led to "disembodiment" and the sensation of being "outside of the body," claims that coincide with reports from trauma studies.

Additionally, Hölzel et al. identified gray matter activation in the posterior cingulate cortex (PCC), an area of the brain responsible for "the integration of self-referential stimuli in the emotional and autobiographical context of one's own person" (8). The cues in MBSR training suggest a return to the phenomena noticed in the present moment; thus structural change in this area infers a compliance with the meditation protocol. Students experiencing trauma are predisposed to hypervigilance and/or withdrawal. Mediating arousal with mindfulness addresses the overwhelm.

The hippocampus, prefrontal cortex, TPJ, and PCC form a brain network in which autobiographical information is not fixed but rather fluid, working "adaptively to enable the perception of alternative perspectives" (Hölzel et al., 2011, 8). This capacity for plurality, cognitive empathy, and self-awareness strengthens the case for incorporating contemplative pedagogies into mainstream education. Not only are students waking to the "self" but also to the "other," and just as meditation yokes the body and mind, so, too, does it reconcile the Other/other. The critical witnessing detailed in chapter 6 can be supported by contemplative practice; based on this premise, we call for further research in collective trauma and mindfulness.

> If you think, "I breathe," the "I" is extra. There is no you to say "I." What we call "I" is just a swinging door which moves when we inhale and when we exhale. It just moves; that is all. When your mind is pure and calm enough to follow this movement, there is nothing: no "I," no world, no mind nor body; just a swinging door.
>
> —(*Zen Mind, Beginner's Mind*, Shunryu Suzuki, 1980, 29)

When left alone waiting in an MRI machine, participants in Farb et al. (2007) turned to their favorite subject: "me." These participants are not unique as "mindwandering" or getting lost in one's thoughts (clinically called stimulus independent thinking), often resulting in a trip into the "story of me" (as described by psychologist Willian James). "Me stories" are fine and can be reflective, engaging, interesting, and fulfilling, until they are not, until they turn into rumination, reinforce implicit bias, and/or promote habitual compliance with social scripts reflecting privileged norms. In short, "me stories" provide a sense of self: "a continuity of identity over time" (Farb et al., 2007, 313).

Farb et al. (2007) stretches across time to unpack the claims of William James (1890), founder of American psychology, by also acknowledging the "I": the self that is attending to the present moment. Farb et al. (2007) used an fMRI to examine dual neural activity in the default mode network during narrative focus (NF) versus experiential focus (EF) in nonmeditators and meditators. NF constructs the identity—a sense of self—over time. It fills in the spaces between events to create a cohesive account of "me." EF reflects a self that arrives in awareness of the present moment—the "I"—as is in the now. Farb et al. (2007) reinforced previous research by finding that the narrative focus engaged with more neural networks in the linguistically mediated and cognitive-affective parts of the brain (interesting in the context of trauma because of the tendency for Broca's region to shut down, limiting access to verbal content as discussed in chapter 2), whereas the experiential focus lit up the somatovisceral parts of the brain. Meditators (versus nonmeditators) in this study spent more of their time in experiential focus—attending to their body and mind as they waited in the MRI machine—as opposed to narrative focus in which they rehearsed for the future or revisited the past. Interestingly, Farb et al. (2007) discovered that meditators who focused attentional awareness on the breath, the body, the present, were able to uncouple and dissociate this neural network. They were able to uncouple their stories about pain, illness, anxiety, and suffering from their momentary experience of pain, illness, anxiety, and suffering. Just as I realized that I was not my worst thought (or my best thought), they realized that "I" was not my disease, pain, or suffering.

Corroborating the gray matter activation in the prefrontal cortex found in Hölzel et al. (2011), Farb et al. (2007) revealed those navigating their autobiographical information in the narrative focus lighting up the prefrontal cortex whereas those existing in experiential focus were lighting up the viscerosomatic areas such as the insula, the secondary somatosensory cortex, and inferior parietal lobule. Participants in both groups could be found attending to their emotional and cognitive regulation (NF), as well as to their somatic awareness (EF): they were in their mind-body and their body-mind or as Varela would say, "embodied mind."

While practicing mindfulness can dissociate these two neural networks—suspend the narrative from the experience—so, too, can trauma. According to Bessel van der Kolk, memories can change over time, but flashbacks cannot. A person who has been traumatized is locked in the flashback, living it in the present tense over and over again. Lanius et al. (2020) investigated the sense of self after trauma by also tapping into the autobiographical and self-referential space of the default mode network. At rest, participants with post-traumatic stress injury showed diminished activity in the prefrontal cortex (the narrative focus), which correlated with subject reports that they felt lost or didn't know themselves or could no longer be themselves. Lanius et al. (2020) inferred that:

> reduced DMN functional connectivity may promote clinical disturbances in self related processes during rest in PTSD, which can include guilt, shame, or remorse emotional experiences, as well as alterations in perceptual experiences, including self-perceptions of body awareness that are perturbed during moments of depersonalization and/or derealization. (4)

For the student who has unprocessed trauma, the simple "tell me about yourself" question on the first day of class (low stakes) or the college admissions essay prompt (high stakes) can induce overwhelm. I can see their faces now and the absence of their faces when they don't return to class.

Hölzel et al. (2011) and Farb et al. (2007) made visible the invisible through topology and imaging, whereas Kerr et al. (2011) used writing—in the form of meditation diaries—to investigate default network mode. Collecting, coding, and analyzing meditation diaries from a randomized clinical trial of MBSR participants, Kerr et al. (2011) were less concerned with what (content) the entries discussed and more with how (form) the posts were constructed: how did they describe their experience of practicing mindfulness meditation *and* how did this description, content, and style change over time? Once the journals were recorded and submitted, each entry was coded as either "reactive" or "reperceiving": "reactivity" (defined in the study as "Reactivity or automaticity involves responding to experiences with reactive thoughts, emotions and behaviors triggered by prior conditioning and habits") or "reperceiving" ("mindfulness practitioners are said to learn to 'disidentify' from present experiences, view them from a novel, 'observing' vantage point and reduce reactivity") (82). In short, the study asked: were participants operating not just out of habitual thought but also out of attachment to the habitual thoughts, sensations, and emotions, or were they open to alternate perspectives and thus to shifting perception? Could the thoughts be transformed; could the thoughts be transformative? Kerr et al. (2011) tested the framework of reperceiving offered by Shapiro et al. (2005); the implications of this research could demonstrate Teasdale's (1999) "suggestion that mindfulness may foster 'metacognition' (the awareness of one's own thoughts as thoughts) that allows participants to reduce their tendency to ruminate on negative experiences" (82).

The study found that by weeks six to seven, participants recorded their thoughts with "greater clarity, detail and less generality," and by the conclusion, all participants had progressed (in varying degrees) at assuming the "observing attitude toward their own experience" (86). While many of the participants did not change how they felt about their illness, pain, or suffering, they did change their relationship to it: "By observing these ruminative and catastrophizing cognitions non-judgmentally, patients begin to strengthen their 'observing selves' (Deikman, 1982), and realize that their negative thoughts and depression are not really them" (90). By not being attached to the presence or outcomes of thoughts, meditators could see thinking as thinking (and feeling as feeling); the core sense of self was not threatened by new experiences or environments but rather available to them.

The implications of this in the English classroom include researchers who operate with intellectual humility, discussion participants who offer vulnerability and cognitive empathy, and reader-writers who approach the page with receptivity. This is a space where diverse thinking and thus ethical awareness is possible. The divisiveness that arises when attachment to thoughts is associated with identity (consider the political-social identity during contentious election years) can be dissolved, and conversation can begin.

In Lanius (2020), PTSD participants claimed, "'I do not know who I am,' or, 'I feel like I have stopped existing'" (5). While Kerr et al. (2011) has been analyzed in the context of the value for participants with depression and anxiety, how might this framework be applied in a mindfulness intervention for PTSD participants? How does the dissociation of body from mind and self from experience after trauma show up in the pages of our students' writing? What might they record on the page that shows their reactivity or reperceiving of the thoughts, feelings, and somatic memories that accompany traumatic events?

Kerr et al. (2011) identified another significant discrimination in the diaries that catalyzed their future mind-body research: "participants found the task of developing an observing perspective easier to carry out when focused on somatic sensations, perhaps because the body feelings that they focused on were so concrete and tangible" (90). This finding resonates with the "show, don't tell" descriptive writing assigned early in our students' careers and semesters. When evaluated in the context of mindfulness, this could serve as an entry point for English teachers hoping to create embodied writing curriculums. Asking students to claim their right to be here by giving agency to the thoughts, sensations, and emotions revealed in attention to the body (breath) in the present moment (on purpose and without judgment) can be empowering. It is an embodied Burkean parlor: if you have a body, please, stand up (or sit in) and be seen and heard. From an equity perspective, this traverses traditional knowledge gaps caused by lack of access to resources. The potential for using embodied writing to develop metacognition, meta-awareness, and contemplation—holding complex, contradictory ideas—has value in curriculums that privilege critical thinking.

Disciplining our attentional focus on the body (the breath) in mindfulness meditation can create the neuroplasticity needed to break habitual scripts about ourselves and others—*the way it has been, should be, ought to be, if only*—thus providing an access point for addressing implicit bias and deconstructing stereotypes that perpetuate master narratives and show up in everything from policy (systemic) to microaggressions (individual). Varela, Kabat-Zinn, and Trungpa all recognize the quantum nature of meditation: it is both building attentional focus (particles) and watching what insight arises (waves). In writing, we say the details should drive the narrative, and the narrative should discern the details: the words spill forth and bite the topography of the page.

Kerr et al. (2013) reminds us that just as the study of Buddhism begins in the body (with the attentional focus of the breath), so, too, does mindfulness start with the body: "body-focused attentional practice in ST-Mindfulness enhances localized attentional control over the 7–14Hz alpha rhythm that is thought to play a key role in regulating sensory input to sensory neocortex and in enhancing signal-to-noise properties across the neocortex" (2). Farb et al. (2007) noted the distinction between the extended (narrative focus) self and the momentary (experiential focused) self in the default mode network where autobiographical information and memory processing occurs. Meditators were able to decouple the self-referential dualism. Kerr et al. (2013) offered the answer to how: by focusing attention somatically—in rather than on the body—meditators were able to turn down the noise of the narrative mindwandering story-making brain (prefrontal cortex) and turn up the volume on the thalamocortical and viscerosomatosensory cortex. Meditators didn't just tune out their ruminating doom and gloom thoughts or aggrandizing self-revelries (reactivity—Kerr et al. 2011), but changed their relationship to these thoughts (reperceiving—Kerr et al. 2011).

Being able to discriminate and differentiate the flood of sensory information is what keeps people from feeling overwhelmed, and because this process works as a neuronal network, it frees up essential working memory to perform higher-order cognitive tasks and emotional regulation. The meditator's ability to feel (with the breath) the inside edge of the left big toe, then the pinky toe, then each of the toes between—the opening cue for the MBSR body scan—helps prime the gates of the sensory information flood and turns down the volume on narrative thought so that the participant can be present and nonjudgmental. Narrative thought is busy dabbling with the past and dreaming (or worrying) about the future; suspending it during somatic attentional focus can disrupt the "me story" long enough to feel connected, available, and open to the experiencing moment. For those who suffer from anxiety and depression, this break from rumination and obsession can feel liberating.

Returning to Lanius (2020), people struggling with a sense of self after trauma often desire:

> re-establishing, or establishing for the first time, a sense of self that is continuous across time and into the future has been a focus of treatment for trauma-related disorders for decades (Allen, 1995; Herman, 1992; van der Kolk, 2015). More

specifically, overcoming the fragmentary, or the timeless nature of traumatic memories, increasing emotional awareness, and helping individuals to reclaim [their] body are critical components of both present- and past-centered therapies . . . *[of which mindfulness intervention is listed]* and mirror eloquently the functions of an intact DMN. (5)

People who have experienced trauma want to feel "whole," and they want that wholeness reflected in the coherence of their story. According to Jon Kabat-Zinn (and the great Tibetan and Zen Buddhism masters who have established this for the past two millennia), we are already whole (even when traumatized). Mindfulness is waking up to that wholeness.

We propose that embodied writing can provide our traumatized students with a satisfaction greater than reductionist coherence or Band-Aid platitudes. Stories satisfy, but authentic, embodied stories fulfill. Contemplative writing engenders the resilience of the mind and neuroplasticity of the brain to see with meta-awareness the rewiring trauma has caused in the brain, to reconcile with metacognition the process in which the rewiring has altered cognition and emotion, and to offer a radical self-love to every part of the body—from the inside edge of the big left toe to the outside edge of the right ear.

When we ask our students to share a personal narrative or to reflect on their human experience—sense of self—we best return to Varela's definition of reflection:

> By embodied we mean reflection in which body and mind have been brought together. What this formulation intends to convey is that reflection is not just on experience, but reflection is a form of experience itself—and that reflective form of experience can be performed with mindfulness/awareness. When reflection is done in that way, it can cut the chain of habitual thought patterns and preconceptions such that it can be an open-ended reflection, open to possibilities other than those contained in one's current representations of the life space. We call this form of reflection mindful, open-ended reflection. (27)

Trauma and Mindfulness

Chapter 2 recollects the experience of a student (Alison) being triggered in the classroom. Chapter 3 reveals the mechanisms at play (the neuroscience of trauma), and chapter 5 demonstrates through literary characters what trauma and survivors of trauma look like on the page. In this chapter, we draw comparisons between the way both trauma and mindfulness disrupt our relationship to narrative, to self, to normative scripts. We can frame trauma as the "site of stress" and mindfulness as the "site of growth"—but we shouldn't. Because it's not that simple. Taking an embodied approach to trauma and mindfulness requires that we confront the function of power, control, and choice. The disruption of self-narrative (me) and narrative-self (I) in trauma is an uninvited or unexpected shearing force that splits, ruptures, fragments, or tears. Control and choice are surrendered to the power of the person-object-environment-condition in which trauma is enacted. The interruption of habitual thoughts, rumination, or normative scripts in mindfulness meditation is an invited, intentional state that uncouples, dissociates, tears, or defamiliarizes. The meditator surrenders control and choice to sit with the self and Other in the present. What defines the space between violence and liberation, overpowered and empowered, overwhelm and insight? How do mindfulness cues like "surrender" threaten the trauma survivor? What happens on the cushion when the body—the one keeping the score—breathes the meditator back into the physiological state they experienced during trauma? Where does the mind follow and fall and fail and reach?

Just as Alison stood up and walked out of the classroom or Taylor crumpled their rough draft freewrite into the bottom of their bag, both students took back control not of their mind-body in the moment of trauma but rather of the processing, reperceiving, reckoning of it. Likewise, when Alison drafts and sends her email, and Taylor pops in for office hours (or doesn't), the potential for an empowering experience exists. It is then that we, as English instructors, must show up to do the work (chapters 2 and 10). Just as we asked ourselves in chapter 5 how we can teach literature that includes trauma and trauma survivors without exposing our students who have experienced trauma to harm, we pause to question here how can we include mindfulness practices with our students. David Treleaven, psychotherapist, trauma professional, and mindfulness instructor, started offering teacher trainings after he experienced his own retraumatization during a meditation retreat. Treleaven, in the no-charge, on-demand webinar *The Truth about Mindfulness and Trauma: How to Mitigate Risks and Promote Healing for Trauma Survivors* (2018) warns:

> Unbeknownst to many, mindfulness practice can exacerbate trauma symptoms. By asking someone to pay close, sustained attention to their inner world, people struggling with trauma can experience flashbacks, dissociation, and even retraumatization. This means that as practitioners, we can unintentionally lead people into the heart of wounds that require more than mindful attention to heal.

Due to overwhelming response to his TSM program, he published *Trauma-Sensitive Mindfulness* (2018). While Treleaven's work focuses on individual experiences and teacher-mediated interventions, the teachings and research of Mushin Ikeda and Helen Weng address collective trauma through intersectional neuroscience. Resmaa Menaken's *My*

Grandmother's Hands (2017) situates the collective trauma in the individual body, contributing to the conversation an understanding of how somatic memory and mindful storytelling can expose, confront, and reconcile racialized trauma.

Incidentally, many of the concerns raised in chapter 1 about the way trauma survivors show up in our classrooms and the recommendations made in chapter 4 about relational teaching (creating healthy relationships and supportive classrooms) apply here. Chapter 2 identified the role that trauma narrative scripts played in the treatment of Bessel van der Kolk's patients. Likewise, meditation scripts—the language used to prompt, cue, plant seeds, and guide—participants should consider 1) *Diversity, Inclusivity, and Accessibility*—who is in the room today, and is the language I am using oppressive, exclusionary, unclear, or antiquated (especially if you are reading a translated or older text)?; 2) *Invitational and Empowering*—does the language I am using invite participants to the task (to say yes), give permission to honor their own bodies and experience (to say no)?; 3) *Trust and Respect*—does the language I am using create trust in both the competence of the leader and the readiness of the participant and demonstrate respect by acknowledging the dignity of the meditator's experience?; and 4) *Compassion and Nonjudgment*—does the language encourage nonjudgment of self and others to reduce the arousal of shame and guilt associated with trauma as well as to inspire compassion for self and others?

The body scan (practiced in MBSR) should offer modifications for trauma survivors, including not requiring the participants to close their eyes (rather, rest them on an object in the room) and in alignment with Kerr et al. (2011), remind meditators to use their bodies to ground their experience; encourage them to press their feet (or seat or hands) into the ground: I am here now; here is safe.

All the activities presented in chapter 6 for embodied writing exercises and mindfulness practices include prompts designed with trauma-sensitive mindfulness principles. Turn to chapter 6 to engage with mindfulness practices specific to the English classroom. (Turn to chapter 10 for exercises oriented toward English teachers and communities of instructors.)

Conclusions

Critical thinking is at the core of most English curricula. Contemplative practice can enrich and enact critical thinking, reading, and writing by encouraging students to arrive at the text with nonjudgment, to read for discovery with comfort in disrupting scripts, to return their attention to the word-page-task when it wanders, and to reconcile their present experience with the larger context of human experience. Rather than think about the English classroom or the written assignment as places to "heal" trauma, we propose disrupting the power-over perspective of fixed/broken, clean/messy, Traumatized/traumatized, or healed/injured and reframing the conversation to include an understanding of how the mind-body works, so that instructors and students can recognize when and how (not necessarily why) a trauma response is triggered in what they are reading, discussing, or writing. Equipping students with the skills and opportunities to exercise choice—*is this the right-place, right-time for me to consume these materials or produce this writing*—restores the experience of connection, safety, and dignity compromised by trauma (chapters 2 and 8). The praxis implications for mindfulness meditation in exposing, addressing, and understanding implicit bias as well as somatic mindfulness in fractured bodies, hearts, and communities are inspiring. By incorporating mindfulness into trauma literacy, we are saying yes to an equitable, empathetic, and empowered classroom. Changing the culture and climate of the classroom begins the necessary work of acknowledging the politics of trauma (chapter 10). Where words—trigger warning—have failed to address the complexity of teaching in a trauma-exposed society, we offer relational gestures (chapter 4), trauma-sensitive reading and writing activities (chapter 6), and mindfulness practices (chapter 9) to cultivate brave spaces where our students are respected and their trauma is dignified.

Chapter 9: Questions for Reflection

1. Consider testing out Ken McLeod's attentional exercise by beholding a flower. Watch your thoughts, sensations, and emotions rise and resolve. Are you strolling down memory lane? Planning the rest of your day? Situated in the contours of the petals? What do you notice about what you notice?
2. Recall a time when your self-narrative was disrupted. Was it "shattered" by trauma? Defamiliarized through art? Suspended in mindfulness? Explore the thoughts, sensations, and emotions that arise as you reflect on the experience. Would you consider this a moment of stress, growth, or something else?
3. Practicing mindfulness with our students requires us to be vulnerable and comfortable with the uncomfortable. Currently, where do you weigh in on this spectrum of "ready" to "no way"? Does the culture/community at your school support mindfulness in the classroom or do you anticipate resistance or skepticism? How might you respond to a student challenge or administrative pushback when embodying contemplative practices in the curriculum?

10

Chapter 10: Showing Up to Do the Work

While teachers enter the classroom at the beginning of the year with nothing more than a roster of names (and perhaps a bit of gossip assigned here and there), they leave the space with a collection of impressions, truths, stories, and questions. We are not impervious to the gun violence, global pandemic, police brutality, weather events, border disputes, cyberstalking, hate crimes, mass incarceration, body shaming, food insecurity, and drug abuse that marks the bodies, hearts, and minds of our students. We see it, hear it, feel it, and live it, too. In a landscape of roadside memorials, we as instructors of writing hold the space for critical witnessing and authentic counternarratives. Holding the space is exhausting. This chapter promotes writing as healing by offering contemplative arts practices to engage instructors and narrative medicine techniques to fortify communities of instructors. Narrative medicine works with practitioners exposed to chronic trauma to cultivate deep listening and self-awareness through exercises in attention, representation, and affiliation. Preventing demoralization and building community are at the heart of this work.

Waves are the practice of water
— Shunryu Suzuki, *Zen Mind, Beginner's Mind*

While chapter 9, "Trauma, Memory, and Narrative," detailed how the neuroscience of meditation, coupled with the cognitive science of memory, can be used to explore language as a construct that can disrupt or perpetuate habitual thinking (the attachment to our stories about self and Other), this section offers contemplative practices and narrative medicine exercises to help instructors employing a trauma-informed pedagogy develop a self-care routine. We move from theory to embodiment before a praxis of trauma can be adopted.

I would like to say that while I was standing at the edge of the water feeling the shore break pull the sand away from my feet—body weight settling into earth—only to return and push it back up until my ankle bones and the shells that raked them where indistinguishable, until the bones in my ear—incus-stapes-malleus—were undulating rhythmically with the ocean articulating secrets of the sea, that this beautiful metaphor for the horrible storm inside my head just came to me. Delivered. A ship. The sky. That would be a great story, but it would not be the truth. No, I was sitting in my car waiting for my therapist to call me up—respecting all the COVID rules—writing frantically on the back of my last appointment card because I forgot my journal, didn't do my therapy homework, and desperately wanted to chuck my phone in a dumpster. I scribbled on the card, figuring I would never be able to read it anyway—the permanence of the pen to page gave way—and it freed up a space, a beat. That is when it came to me. I had not had a "deep" thought (or a deep think) in months.

I was standing in what Rachel Carson would call the littoral zone—"the edge of the sea, where only the most hardy and adaptable survive"—letting the waves break against me over and over. A wave can only break in water that is one-half its depth: an eight-foot wave breaks in four feet of water. When the bottom of the sea shifts and redistributes the sand, bars form, invisible to those on the shore except for these breaks. This was my mind—a shifting bottom.

Every news notification, every email ping, every call from the other room—every interruption—was breaking across my bow. I had shallow thoughts—so many shallow thoughts so close together I started to splinter. I was exhausted. And I was not alone. When I looked over, we were all lined up, cringing against IT as one: the contagion of fear and the fear of contagious—anxiety hooked through our eyes, we towed and dragged that line together. We were exhausted.

It was not *not* thinking (frankly, that would have been delightful); it was thinking and thinking and thinking and not getting "anywhere."

My dad taught me this young: *While the shoreline seems safe because the water is shallow, and you feel like you have some control with your feet on the ground, the real protection is to get out past the breakers—to go beyond—to the deep water. When you are tired, let the saltwater carry you. Feel yourself float with it, in it, to it.*

I wanted to be carried, to be connected, to float. That's what was missing: my deep water. But it takes time to swim out to the deep water and then swim back, and let's face it, who has time like that to spare? As a mom juggling family and career during a pandemic, I felt lucky if I brushed my teeth and took a shower in the same day.

Kris, you have to stand here and count the waves in a set—figure out how many and how close together—then you will know how much time to hold your breath and how to get out past the breakers. And don't forget it, 'cause you'll need it to get you back in.

The way to trick time was through timing—a shift in perception that comes as a shift in attention—I could feel the container and use it to move me. I could channel the energy around me to draw me out of this shallow thinking, shallow breathing, shallow feeling spot and to move to the deep water. Anticipating the moment the feet can no longer reach the bottom feels so much different than being in the moment—lifted, the saltwater cradles the form and resets the center of levity.

There is suddenly space to move and time to breathe and the shore looks so far away—all that exhaustion left on the sand. Mihaly Csikszentmihalyi, a positive psychologist and creativity and happiness expert, would call this optimal flow—the experience of being so present in the moment that there is no hesitation and no anticipation, just nowness and with-ness. In the deep waters of the ocean, one does not feel the breaking against the shore; in the deep waters of the mind-body, thought and sensation are unattached from suffering. Time stretches, intercostal muscles stretch, joints surrender, and cilia receive: we open ourselves up to ourselves. And because we listened and remembered how many waves were in a set, when it is time to go back to the shore, instead of fighting to avoid the crashing breakers, instead, we ride them in—feeling the speed and force of the sea as it barrels us back to safety. No fighting and thrashing and clinging.

You can come up now, the text read. I had been "gone" –off in the deep thoughts—for only five minutes, but it felt like an hour (like an hour and a good nap!). Then my therapist and I spent the session exploring ways I could swim out to my deep water—to have my deep thoughts and my deep thinks—even though everything about the pandemic resisted these spaces for me.

Establishing a contemplative practice cultivates the disciplined interiority to help us both weather the storm—the traumatic events that disrupt—as well as to manage the daily surf—the series of interruptions. Trauma can keep us feeling stuck, returning over and over to it like the perpetual shore break. How can we rewrite this line? How can we create space—access the deep waters of our body-mind-heart—to suspend the breaking? To create room for the salt to help us heal our physical, emotional, mental, and spiritual wounds? How can we afford ourselves the room to play and risk and grieve and flail and fail and float and grow that we so generously scaffold into assignments for our students? Contemplative practices can change our perception of time, regulate our inner narrative, and condition our sensation of attention so that we can navigate the waters of personal and professional life when trauma shows up uninvited at the classroom door or on the page.

Contemplative Practices: Doing the Inner Work of Trauma-Informed Pedagogy

You do not have to be good.
You do not have to walk on your knees
for a hundred miles through the desert repenting.
You only have to let the soft animal of your body
love what it loves.
— Mary Oliver, 'Wild Geese"

In chapter 7 "Responding to and Assessing Student Writing," we emphasized the need for instructors to give feedback on student work in a healthy place between "enmeshed" (responding only to their pain and revelation) and "disengaged" (responding only to the grammar and mechanics on the page). Doing the inner work will help to fortify the instructor from inhabiting their students' trauma, projecting their trauma onto their students, and judging their students based on their own trauma and how they would have "handled" the disclosed experience.

If the instructor has experienced trauma, then they should seek out a mental health professional; this is part one (the foundation) of doing the inner work.

This section offers some contemplative practices that can be used as daily maintenance for working in a trauma-sensitive pedagogy and to build resilience for future trauma (part two). In addition to supporting instructors exploring their own trauma response and narrative, they can also provide opportunities for teachers to experience, notice, and examine with curiosity and courage their own implicit biases: where did that come from? Why was I attracted or repelled by that thought, sensation, feeling, image, or word? What messages are encoded in me, and which ideologies transmit these stereotypes, archetypes, and assumptions? To hold brave spaces for students, instructors need their own space to listen in to what arises when they sit with themselves.

Holding nonjudgment of thoughts, sensations, and feelings of "self" takes practice; it is not inherently Western and thus is not always supported in American culture and education. If we don't want to "dump" our trauma onto our students, then we also need the clear perception and awareness of our bias and lens before we choose to offer the lifelines our students call for on the page.

These exercises are based on my training in the MFA writing and poetics program at Naropa University (a Buddhist college founded by Chogyam Trungpa Rinpoche), Brown University's contemplative pedagogy summer program (with Catherine Kerr, Willoughby Britton, Harold Roth, and Jared Lindahl), somatic yoga teacher training (with Bobbie Ellis and Deborah Metzger), and Bachelors of Science Degree in exercise science with minors in biology and psychology from Rutgers University coupled with my eighteen-year personal meditation practice, fifteen-year somatic yoga and embodied movement instruction, and eleven years of teaching college-level writing with a contemplative pedagogy.

They employ a blend of John Kabat-Zinn's Mindfulness Based Stress Reduction techniques, Chogyam Trungpa Rinpoche's Shambhala art/dharma art practices, Reed Bye's contemplative poetics, Allen Ginsberg's mind writing slogans, Jack Kerouac's spontaneous prose, and contemplative pedagogy research from Harold Roth, Willoughby Britton, Jared Lindahl, and Mirabai Bush.

Included on the following pages is a graphic that organizes the instruction for, benefits of, and triggers present for each type of contemplative exercise offered. Contemplative silence practices help to condition the mind: 1) to sit with uncertainty, saturation, boredom, and complexity; 2) to turn down the noise and turn up the focal point—to fine-tune the attention; and 3) to identify patterns in thought, attachment to outcomes, and implicit bias.

They help us learn to listen to what is there, when it is there, and to let go of it so that we can be here. Contemplative writing practices help to make visible what is invisible through the representative act of writing. They can distill truth from the collection of facts. We pose that these practices work together to create moments of inhale and exhale: spaces for the instructor to play, experiment, fail, and breathe, to acknowledge what they have witnessed and how it affects them, and to recalibrate, recenter, and restore.

CONTEMPLATIVE SILENCE

BEHOLDING

Script/ Instruction	Benefits/Outcomes
Beholding "Wisdom does not inspect, but behold. We must look a long time before we can see."— Henry David Thoreau Choose a painting to sit with for five minutes each day for several weeks. Sit with the painting. Return to this painting. Soften your edges around judgment, narration, or interpretation and strengthen your focus on observation and awareness. The practice of beholding requires suspending judgment, interpretation, and evaluations of the beheld to answer the question, "What do you see?" This contemplative practice cultivates awareness, receptivity, and "true perception" (Trungpa). Reflection Part I: What do you see? What remains? Part II: Describe your experience with beholding. Note your reactions/responses/ reflections/feelings/observations. What personal, interpersonal, environmental, or cultural factors influenced your experience? Part III: Explore the relationship between awe (or engraced) and the act of beholding.	• Sitting in Appreciation • Sitting without Judgment • Subverting Interpretation/Narrative/ Meaning Making • Cultivating Observation Skills • Practicing Awareness • Subverting Objectification • Suspending Bias/Preference/Aversion/ Attraction/Attachment **Triggers/ Reactions** Choose a painting that does not contain content associated with common triggers: gun violence, rape, abuse, or war. Listen to your body's emotional response to the artwork—to sitting in silence with the artwork—and note if you are feeling triggered, uncomfortable, or charged.

CONTEMPLATIVE SILENCE

FOCUSED ATTENTION

Script/ Instruction

- I am human.
- Write down a word or short (two or three words) phrase that sets your intention, what you would like to cultivate or focus on.
- Repeat it on both the inhale and the exhale.
- I (inhale) am (hold) human (exhale).
- Sync breath to word.
- If your mind-body wanders, return it to the focus—the word.

Benefits/Outcomes

- We choose what we want to cultivate
- We acknowledge what distracts or deters
- We recognize the value of AWARENESS & DISCERNMENT (cell-signaling . . . membranes)
- We discipline or practice discernment by sitting in focused attention
- Benefits: improve attention span, receptivity, tranquility, and peace
- Calm comes over time . . .
- Rooted in shamatha meditation

Triggers/ Reactions

Listen to your body's emotional response to the practice—to sitting in silence in the practice—and note if you are feeling triggered, uncomfortable, or charged. Please, feel free to soften your gaze.

CONTEMPLATIVE SILENCE

Open Monitoring

Script/Instruction

Open Monitoring Instruction

- Find a comfortable seat.
- Soften the gaze by staring at a single point in front of you.
- Bring attention to the inside edge of the nose.
- Breathe in and breathe out naturally.
- Locate the place in the nose where you notice the breath.
- Label this breathing. Notice the moments when your attention wanders away from breathing.
- To monitor, notice the shift, be present with it, label it: THOUGHT, SENSATION, or EMOTION.
- Add in an awareness of TIME: Label THOUGHT, SENSATION, or EMOTION as PAST (memory/residue), PRESENT (experiencing/witnessing), FUTURE (planning/fantasizing)
- Let the those things recede and return to BREATH.
- Repeat for five to ninety years.

REFLECTION

"Never mind what I have been taught. Forget about theories and prejudices and stereotypes. I want to understand the true nature of life. I want to know what this experience of being alive really is. I want to apprehend the true and deepest qualities of life, and I don't want to just accept somebody else's explanation. I want to see it for myself." —Gunaratana

The practice of open monitoring requires suspending judgment, interpretation, and evaluations of the beheld to answer the question, "What do you see?" This contemplative practice cultivates awareness, receptivity, and "true perception" (Trungpa).

Part I: Where am I? When am I? What remains: breathing, thoughts, sensations, feelings, and past, present, future. Where/when did you spend your open monitoring time today? How much was spent in "breathing"?

Part II: Describe your experience with open monitoring. Note your reactions/responses/reflections/feelings/observations. What personal, interpersonal, environmental, or cultural factors influenced your experience?

Part III: "We are not paying enough attention to notice that we are not paying attention."—Gunaratana. What are you attending to and avoiding, nurturing and neglecting, or holding or withholding?

Benefits/Outcomes

- Stimulates creativity and innovation;
- Encourages acceptance via acknowledgement;
- Promotes self- and Other awareness;
- Dismantles bias, stereotypes, and pity;
- Delivers TRUTH

Triggers/ Reactions

Listen to your body's emotional response to the practice—to sitting in silence in the practice—and note if you are feeling triggered, uncomfortable, or charged.

If focusing on the breath is producing heightened anxiety or physical discomfort, bring your attention instead to the weight of the hands or the soles of the feet. Please, feel free to soften your gaze instead of closing your eyes.

CONTEMPLATIVE SILENCE

Close Reading (Lectio Divina)

Identify a passage from a text that stands out to you—one that engages, intrigues, speaks, questions your attention. You may also consider a koan or paradox for this exercise. Write out the quote on a notecard. Read it three times to commit it (words and/or essence) to memory. Turn over the notecard and write your experience with the words, thoughts, sensations, and feelings carried in the language. Note aversion/attraction; avoidance/fixation; pleasure/critique; visceral/conceptual; question/answer; etc. On separate occasions, return to the card and repeat the exercise. Reflection: How does your understanding of, appreciation for, and experience with the language change over time? What remains the same? What associations arise and fall away?

Focused Freewrite

Select a word, image, question, or idea. Write it on the top of the page. Freewrite for five to ten minutes. During this time, record all ideas, thoughts, sensations that arise:

- No editing, no revising, just writing. Keep your hand (or typing fingers) moving.
- If your writing shifts away from the prompt, attend to the thought and then return to the prompt without judgment—notice where you go and how you return.
- If you feel the need to "look something up," don't. Instead, write a note to self in the freewrite: look up X later . . .
- Let ideas surface, develop, shift, and fall away without attachment.
- Watch and record without judgment.

Open Freewrite

Come to the blank page with your busy mind-body and unpack. During this time, record all ideas, thoughts, sensations that arise:

- No editing, no revising, just writing. Keep your hand (or typing fingers) moving.
- If you feel the need to "look something up," don't. Instead, write a note to self in the freewrite: look up X later . . .
- If you feel the need to talk to your neighbor, don't. Instead, write down the things you are dying to tell your neighbor (the story!!!!)
- Let ideas surface, develop, shift, and fall away without attachment.
- Watch and record without judgment.
- You are creating a primordial soup. Incubation to follow.

Narrative Medicine: Preventing Burnout and Building Community

Dr. Rita Charon of Columbia University is a pioneer and leader in the field of narrative medicine. Dr. Charon and her team of arts, humanities, and medical professionals have been training Columbia Medical School cohorts, offering workshops to support healthcare practitioners, and certifying narrative medicine program leaders since the 1980s. Narrative medicine started as a practice for helping medical professionals cultivate empathetic listening skills to better understand the stories their patients were disclosing to them, and thus to improve not just their quality of disease management but their overall treatment experience with the patient. Charon et al. also identified the compassion fatigue and desensitization to the pain and suffering of others that plagued busy trauma units and crisis or resource-stricken clinics and patient care centers. Narrative medicine started as a practice in attending to the patient and grew to include taking care of the practitioner. This method has attracted attention in law enforcement, particularly in restorative justice, bias training, and de-escalation training. We move that as trauma and reporting trauma becomes more common in educational settings, educators could benefit from narrative medicine programming.

This section is not designed to teach narrative medicine or to conduct narrative medicine but rather to encourage educators and administrators to consider enlisting and sponsoring narrative medicine programs for employees. While trauma has been shown to isolate and alienate, we pose that narrative medicine can reframe the silent suffering with a community address. Just as we showed that critical witnessing and positionality stories are important ways to support our students in the classroom (chapters 4 and 6), we recommend mirroring these through narrative medicine in the teaching community. Burnout comes not just from feeling fatigued but also from feeling underappreciated or unseen. By encouraging faculty to read, write, and share as a community, a school culture of radical compassion can be curated.

Narrative medicine programming includes: 1) a shared text—poem, story, film, painting, dance, etc., 2) a reflective writing prompt inspired by the shared text, and 3) a period of sharing what was written and listening while suspending judgment and offering observations about the story. The structure of the workshop models the value of close reading and creative writing as skills for stretching empathetic imagination, remaining receptive to stories, and treating people with dignity and care. This type of empathic listening demonstrates vulnerability and builds trust.

Using a shared text to help focus attention, narrative medicine guides participants through the very same close reading skills we teach our literature and writing students (chapter 5). Reflective writing in response to a prompt generated by the shared text reinforces the value of writing as representation: "To write is not only to record or report but also to discover" (Charon, Hermann, and Devlin, 2016, 2). In writing, we dredge up from the subconscious what is invisible and give it a shape—a narrative—to be experienced and examined. "The writer—or painter, composer, filmmaker—achieves, through representation, some aspect of what [they] ha[ve] witnessed or imagined" (Charon, Hermann, and Devlin, 2016, 2). A third and important part of narrative medicine programming, is affiliation. Staci K. Haines, somatic therapy counselor, reminds us that trauma is individual and social, and thus affiliation is an important part of the narrative medicine paradigm. By sharing the spontaneous reflective writing with a cohort, the group can witness one another's trauma and stay receptive, connected, and engaged with and to their community: we are all in this together.

The contemplative exercises shared in the first section of this chapter focused on ways to examine your relationship with yourself (lens, bias, trauma, narrative). The individual was framed as the container for preparation, restoration, reconciliation, and healing. This is necessary, but there is another important vector that needs to be stressed here: the systemic and institutional problems (structure) and the environment in which teaching is happening (school climate). One can practice self-care night and day; however, if the teacher has little support from administrators and parents, few resources to tap into, and structural/hierarchical problems to contend with, then demoralization (and in its extreme burnout) are on the horizon. Americans applaud their athletes, soldiers, leaders, and even students for their grit—the ability to sustain focus and achieve even in the face of adversity, to persevere. It fits neatly in with rugged individualism and the American Dream, and so it is hard to be critical of it, but we must be. And while we are at it, let's decontextualize resilience, as Nkem Ndefo has done in her *Resilience Toolkit* for somatic practitioners.

In an interview with the NEA, Doris Santoro, author of *Demoralization: Why Teachers Leave the Profession They Love and How They Can Stay*, not only noted the distinction between burnout and demoralization but also emphasized how burnout shames and blames the individual educator for not being able to "make it" in the system rather than addressing the conditions of the system that drain and deplete educators. By over-emphasizing self-care, grit, and resilience in the context of healing and trauma, we keep the conversation fixed on the individual and forget to address the structural and institutional problems that perpetuate stress and trauma.

This is why we recommend narrative medicine programming for educators in high-stress, trauma-laden environments (by the end of 2020, read: all school environments), because it allows for self-care within the community and, through affiliation, creates texts that can undergo close reading—patterns within the group can be pulse checks for the campus climate. Is there resonance or dissonance, accord or discord, and appreciation or demoralization? How is the room read and what is done (or not done) with this information?

While much research has been publicized on post-traumatic stress disorder and how to heal individually, little has been shared on post-traumatic growth and how to heal collectively. During the experience of trauma and the retriggering of trauma, the nervous system shifts into overwhelm (chapters 2 and 9). Restoring baseline or returning to balance constitutes recovery, but we see here an opportunity for more than recovery—for growth. In departments and schools where instructors can practice and share in a trauma-conscious environment, we boldly assert that both individual and systemic transformation is possible. When the same critical witnessing and relational pedagogy that we employ in our classrooms with students is also engaged between administration and instructors, then real growth and change are possible. This section is a call to leaders in education: see us, hear us, be with us, and stop putting the onus for change solely on our very capable, very cope-able shoulders.

In closing, I offer a few narrative medicine workshop examples that showcase the intersection of contemplative, creative, and reflective writing with critical witnessing.

Text (Attention)	Reflective Writing (Representation) & Sharing (Affiliation)
POEM: "The Hill We Climb" by Amanda Gorman	Choose one of the lines from Amanda Gorman's poem to launch your own investigation of the hill (noun/place) and/or the climb (verb/space). Write the line on the top of your page and start freewriting for five minutes straight. Don't stop, edit, think, filter—just let the words pour onto the page. OPTION A: Even as we grieved, we grew . . . OPTION B: If only we are brave enough to . . .

Text (Attention)	Reflective Writing (Representation) & Sharing (Affiliation)
STORY: "The Sky is Gray" by Ernest J. Gaines	"I look at mama and I love my mama. She's wearing that black coat and that black hat and she's looking sad. I love my mama and I want put my arm round her and tell her. But I'm not supposed to do that. She says that's weakness and that's crybaby stuff, and she don't want no crybaby round her . . . I can't ever be scared and I can't ever cry. And that's why I never said nothing 'bout my teeth. It's been hurting me and hurting and hurting me close to a month now, but I never said it, I didn't say it 'cause I didn't want to act like a crybaby, and 'cause I know we didn't have enough money to go have it pulled." (Gaines 84) "When I see people eating, I get hungry; when I see a coat, I get cold." (104) PROMPT: Creatively or reflectively respond to this line from the text: "It's been hurting me and hurting and hurting me [for a long time] now, but I never said it, I didn't say it because . . . "
TEXT: *My Body, My Earth: The Practice of Somatic Archaeology* by Ruby Gibson	"Our bodies, like Earth are the keepers of memory. Just like the Earth contains the historical library of life in its ruins, graves, trees, rocks and oceans, our bodies inherit the archives of our ancestors, in their cells, muscles, blood, and bones. . . . When we wish to examine how we evolved as a culture and a species, we dig in the earth. . . . To examine how each of us evolved as individuals or as family systems, and to explore the social and spiritual influences that have shaped us, we excavate our bodies." (Prompt by Carmen Price, Narrative Medicine Practitioner): Tell the story of your name . . .

Text (Attention)

Girl at Mirror
by Norman Rockwell

Reflective Writing (Representation) & Sharing (Affiliation)

Stretching the Empathetic Imagination
Posture and Attitude

- What does it feel like to arrange your bones in the posture of the child?
- What does it feel like to breathe in that posture?
- What does it feel like to hold your bones there—to use your muscle tissue in that way?
- What thoughts, emotions, or sensations arise as you sit at the mirror with the child?

Reflective Write: What comes up for you while sitting at the "mirror" with the child? What do you notice about her? What do you notice about yourself?

Creative Writing Prompt: Stretching the Empathetic Imagination
Using your field notes from the beholding and embodying exercise as a start, complete this series of creative writing exercises to stretch your imagination and practice deep empathy for this young girl. What does the girl want to tell someone? What stands in the way of her either telling or being heard/understood? Who does she want to tell, and is it the same person as the one she will actually tell? Either set a timer for five minutes per prompt or give yourself a container of 250 words per prompt. Respond in fiction, poetry, hybrid—whatever feels right.

1. Third-person POV: Once upon a time, there was a girl... [tell the story about the girl]
2. Second-person POV: Dear Little Girl, You... [address the child as "you"]
3. First-person POV: This one time when I felt... [step inside the girl's body and tell the story of an emotional truth you both share].
4. First-person POV Reflective: When I sit with the little girl, I... [explore the experience of you sitting with and trying to understand this child...]

Text (Attention)	Reflective Writing (Representation) & Sharing (Affiliation)
POEM: "Social Distancing" by Juan Felipe Herrera	PROMPT: Choose one of the rays/petals/strands to start your own writing. A virus is like an ouroboros—it eats its own tail, it chases its own tale, it tells and is told in circles. What tangent will you explore or what vector will you use as a point of entry to break the circle?
STORY: "A Small, Good Thing" by Raymond Carver	"You probably need to eat something," the baker said. "I hope you'll eat some of my hot rolls. You have to eat and keep going. Eating is a small, good thing in a time like this," he said. (Carver, 28) PROMPT: . . . so I can only imagine what you must be feeling.
 PAINTING: *The Scream* by Edvard Munch	PROMPT: Perspective and Mood Part 1: The Scream What do you notice? Where do you find your attention focusing on/in the painting? Whom? Tell the "story" of the painting from the perspective of the screamer or the bystander or the viewer of the painting (aka you).

<table>
<tr><th>Text (Attention)</th><th>Reflective Writing (Representation) & Sharing (Affiliation)</th></tr>
<tr><td>
PAINTING (Continued): The Two Fridas by Frida Kahlo

Les Demoiselles D'Avignon by Pablo Picasso</td><td>Part 2: The Two Fridas

What do you notice? Where do you find your attention focusing in/on the painting? Whom?

Tell the "story" of the painting from the perspective of one of the Fridas.

Part 3: Les Demoiselles D'Avignon

What do you notice? Where do you find your attention focusing in/on the painting? Whom?

Tell the "story" of the painting from the perspective of one of the women or the bystander/patron.</td></tr>
</table>

Conclusion

And while Alison, Johnny, Suzy, Wendy, Jamil, Tyrelle, Sal, Marty, Rick, Phillipe, Sean, Jennifer, Peter, Andrew, and Taylor are turning up in your classroom, and Sethe, Blanche, Hester, Hamlet, Ophelia, Willy, Amir are arriving on each page, you are showing up to turn those pages, to attune that classroom, and to account for who is present. If you have worried that you will not be able to relate to the type of trauma your students have experienced, then you are not alone; if you are worried that you will relate too closely to the trauma that your students share in the classroom, then you are not alone; if you have asked yourself what is the difference between turning up and showing up, then you are not alone; if you have asked yourself am I turning up or showing up—and gotten different answers on different days—then you are not alone; if you are doing a lot of work—working—then you are not alone; if you are wondering how to do "the work," then you are not alone. Join Adam, Cassie, and Kristen in the teaching trauma literacy roll call: am I *here* yet?

Wouldn't it be easy and tidy if we said the first step in showing up to do the work was acquiring this book, and the second step was reading it? But we know that nothing about trauma is easy or tidy (chapter 1) and teaching is not a one-way street (chapter 4). In Inuit culture, travelers arrange piles of rocks on the path, often in the shape of a human, to simultaneously say to the next person who passes: *you are on the right path and someone was here before you.* We offer these words—this text—and hope that you, too, will then make your own inuksuk to share with our larger English teacher community. We are starting this conversation, but we hope that you will continue it.

While the trigger warning served as a first response to protecting our students and ourselves from the ways in which trauma showed up, unannounced, and scratched the blackboard (chapter 3), we posit that it is time for a new way of addressing and reconciling trauma in our learning communities. Understanding the neuroscience of trauma (chapter 2) and the neuroscience of mindfulness (chapter 9) can help us see the power of the mind-body connection in learning, language, and transformation. If we can see our bodies and minds as texts we can read (chapters 6, 7, and 8) by recognizing the patterns of trauma in those lines we have already read (chapter 5), then the transferability of our skills as English teachers—close reading, critical thinking, active listening, and deep reflection—can be used in a way that is sustainable and meaningful to ourselves and to our profession. Teaching trauma literacy helps prepare not only the instructor but also the students (chapter 4). While Part One, *Consumption,* dignifies trauma—something that requires our immediate attention and care—Part Two, *Declaration,* through assignments (chapter 6), feedback strategies and assessment tools (chapter 7), and examples (chapter 8) dignifies the classroom as a space where it can be bravely witnessed: no invitation necessary, come as you are, we are now here. We close Part Three, *Embodiment* (chapter 10) with a gesture to nourish your own body-mind-spirit and to share this with your community. If you have experienced trauma, we recommend seeking a professional healer (in the modality of your choice) to do the inner work with support.

Caring for yourself dignifies trauma—the way it can spill, project, plant, erupt, freeze not just our body-minds but those who love, live, and work with us, who sit in our classrooms and conference rooms. We also call to action the administrators and leaders in education who need to show up and do the work of dismantling any systemic racist, sexist, ableist, classist, or ageist policies that exacerbate the experience of trauma, exclude or alienate trauma survivors, or resist and demoralize those teaching trauma literacy.

We are not impervious to the gun violence, global pandemic, police brutality, weather events, border disputes, cyberstalking, hate crimes, mass incarceration, body shaming, food insecurity, and drug abuse that marks the bodies, hearts, and minds of our students.

We see it, hear it, feel it, and live it, too.

In a landscape of roadside memorials, we as instructors of English hold the space for critical witnessing and authentic counternarratives.

Holding the space is exhausting.

Contemplative practice builds the "muscle" for meeting adversity and trauma in our personal and professional lives; narrative medicine is the gathering of these muscles together and a reckoning of the system in which they reside. What is the health of the community? How will we coordinate our response? Who will we stand by? Who will stand by us? How can we build a more sustainable teaching practice?

We see you; we hear you; we are with you.

Chapter 10: Questions for Reflection

1. What does your current self-care routine look like, and how did you develop it? How does it serve you? Where do you feel you could use more resources or more support in your own healing process?
2. What types of memorials, messaging, or critical witnessing opportunities are present in your community? What would you like to see more of? Less of? How would you describe the way colleagues and administration respond to crisis, grief, stress, and trauma? Are you satisfied with this response?
3. What was the last art piece you encountered that defamiliarized your thoughts, drew out your emotions, or made you feel connected? What about the piece shakes, settles, or holds you? Take this space to reflectively or creatively respond to the art piece. What remains?

Notes

i. The reader should know that all student names in this book are pseudonyms.

ii. Note that these are not discrete statistics. An individual who suffers physical abuse may also be sexually molested or grow up around alcoholic relatives.

iii. It should also be noted that history teachers face a significant challenge when it comes to teaching trauma-laden content related to slavery, war, political upheaval, race relations, etc. This book will not address history instruction directly, but it is clear to us how teaching history presents analogous complications and opportunities relative to trauma.

iv. It should be noted that these are not necessarily discrete statistics. For instance, a percentage of depressed adolescents are also anxious, etc.

v. Several definitions of adolescence cite a beginning age as early as ten years old and go up to age twenty-five, around the time the brain finishes developing (Curtis, 2015).

Works Cited

Alexander, J. C., Eyerman, R., Giesen, B., Smelser, N. J., & Sztompka, P. (2004). *Cultural trauma and collective identity.* University of California Press.

Allen, J. G. (1995). *Coping with trauma: A guide to self-understanding.* American Psychiatric Pub, Inc.

Angelou, M. (2008). *I know why the caged bird sings.* Penguin.

Arao, B., & Clemens, K. (2013). From safe spaces to brave spaces. In L. Landreman (Ed.), *The art of effective facilitation: Reflections from social justice educators* (pp. 135–150). Stylus Publishing.

Aristotle, Longinus, & Demetrius. (1995). *Aristotle: Poetics. Longinus: On the sublime. Demetrius: On style* (S. Halliwell, W. Fyfe, D. Innes, & W. Roberts, Trans.). Harvard University Press.

Arzy, S., Thut, G., Mohr, C., Michel, C. M., & Blanke, O. (2006). Neural basis of embodiment: Distinct contributions of temporoparietal junction and extrastriate body area. *The Journal of Neuroscience, 26*(31), 8074–8081. https://doi.org/10.1523/JNEUROSCI.0745-06.2006

Babington, A. (2007). *Shell-shock: A history of the changing attitudes to war neurosis.* Pen and Sword Select.

Banitt, S. P. (2012). *The trauma tool kit: Healing PTSD from the inside out.* Quest Books.

Barbezat, D. P., & Bush, M. (2013). *Contemplative practices in higher education: Powerful methods to transform teaching and learning*. Jossey-Bass.

Bartholomae, D., & Elbow, P. (1995). Responses to Bartholomae and Elbow. *College Composition and Communication, 46*(1), 84–92.

Bitsko, R. H., Claussen, A. H., Lichstein, J., Black, L. I., Jones, S. E., Danielson, M. L., Hoenig, J. M., Davis Jack, S. P., Brody, D. J., Gyawali, S., Maenner, M. J., Warner, M., Holland, K. M., Perou, R., Crosby, A. E., Blumberg, S. J., Avenevoli, S., Kaminski, J. W., Ghandour, R. M., & Contributor. (2022). Mental health surveillance among children—United States, 2013–2019. *MMWR Supplements, 71*(2), 1–42. https://doi.org/10.15585/mmwr.su7102a1

Blanke, O., Mohr, C., Michel, C. M., Pascual-Leone, A., Brugger, P., Seeck, M., Landis, T., & Thut, G. (2005). Linking out-of-body experience and self-processing to mental own-body imagery at the temporoparietal junction. *The Journal of Neuroscience, 25*(3), 550–557. https://doi.org/10.1523/JNEUROSCI.2612-04.2005

Blau, S. D. (2003). *The literature workshop: Rethinking the classic problems of instruction.* Heinemann.

Bloom, H. (2003). *Hamlet: Poem unlimited.* Riverhead Books.

Britzman, D. P., & Pitt, A. J. (2004). Pedagogy and clinical knowledge: some psychoanalytic observations on losing and refinding significance. *JAC, 24*(2), 353–374. http://www.jstor.org/stable/20866629

Bruns, C. V. (2011). *Why literature? The value of literary reading and what it means for teaching.* Continuum.

Butler, J. (1994). Contingent foundations: Feminism and the question of "postmodernism." In N. Fraser, *Feminist contentions: A philosophical exchange* (pp. 3–21). Routledge.

Carello, J., & Butler, L. D. (2015). Practicing what we teach: Trauma-informed educational practice. *Journal of Teaching in Social Work, 35*(3), 262–278. https://doi.org/10.1080/08841233.2015.1030059

Carmody, J., Baer, R. A., LB Lykins, E., & Olendzki, N. (2009). An empirical study of the mechanisms of mindfulness in a mindfulness-based stress reduction program. *Journal of Clinical Psychology, 65*(6), 613–626. https://doi.org/10.1002/jclp.20579

Charon, R. (2008). *Narrative medicine: Honoring the stories of illness*. Oxford University Press.

Charon, R., Hermann, N., & Devlin, M. J. (2016). Close reading and creative writing in clinical education: Teaching attention, representation, and affiliation. *Academic Medicine: Journal of the Association of American Medical Colleges, 91*(3), 345–350. https://doi.org/10.1097/ACM.0000000000000827

Christie, D., McFarlane, F., Casdagli, L., & Fredman, G. (2016). Witnessing outsider witnessing: A reciprocal witnessing workshop with young people reclaiming their lives back from pain and fatigue. *Physical Medicine and Rehabilitation Research, 1*(4), 1–6. https://doi.org/10.15761/PMRR.1000122

Cridland-Hughes, S. (2015). Caring critical literacy: The most radical pedagogy you can offer your students. *English Journal, 105*(2), 129–132.

Curtis, A.C. (2015). Defining adolescence. *Journal of Adolescent and Family Health, 7*(2).

Deikman, A. J. (1982). *The observing self: Mysticism and psychotherapy.* Beacon Press.

Dutro, E. (2017). Let's start with heartbreak: The perilous potential of trauma in literacy. *Language Arts, 94*(5), 326–337.

———. (2008). "That's why I was crying on this book": Trauma as testimony in responses to literature. *Changing English, 15*(4), 423–434. https://doi.org/10.1080/13586840802493076

———. (2019). *The vulnerable heart of literacy: Centering trauma as powerful pedagogy.* Teachers College Press.

———. (2011). Writing wounded: Trauma, testimony, and critical witness in literacy classrooms. *English Education, 43*(2), 193–211.

Early, J. S., DeCosta-Smith, M., & Valdespino, A. (2010). Write your ticket to college: A genre-based college admission essay workshop for ethnically diverse, underserved students. *Journal of Adolescent & Adult Literacy, 54*(3), 209–219. https://doi.org/10.1598/JAAL.54.3.6

Epstein, M. (2013, August 3). The trauma of being alive. *The New York Times.* http://www.newyorktimes.com/2013/08/04/opinion/sunday/thetrauma-of-being-alive.html

———. (2014). *The trauma of everyday life.* Hay House.

Farb, N. A., Segal, Z. V., Mayberg, H., Bean, J., McKeon, D., Fatima, Z., & Anderson, A. K. (2007). Attending to the present: Mindfulness meditation reveals distinct neural modes of self-reference. *Social Cognitive and Affective Neuroscience, 2*(4), 313–322. https://doi.org/10.1093/scan/nsm030

Felman, S., & Laub, D. (1991). T*estimony: Crises of witnessing in literature, psychoanalysis, and history.* Taylor and Francis.

Fitzgerald, F. S. (2004). *The Great Gatsby.* Scribner.

Fredrickson, R. (1992). *Repressed memories: A journey to recovery from sexual abuse.* Simon & Schuster.

Friedman, T. (2016). *Thank you for being late: An optimist's guide to thriving in the age of acceleration.* Allen Lane.

Gibran, K. (2020). *The prophet.* Read & Co.

Greene, M. (1988). *The dialectic of freedom.* Teachers College Press.

Gross, N., & Lo, C. (2018). Relational teaching and learning after loss: Evidence from Black adolescent male students and their teachers. *School Psychology Quarterly, 33*(3), 381–389. https://doi.org/10.1037/spq0000285

Hawthorne, N. (2012). *The scarlet letter.* Simon & Brown.

Heer, J. (2015, May 20). Generation PTSD: What the 'trigger warning' debate is really about. *The New Republic.* https://newrepublic.com/article/121866/history-ptsdand-evolution-trigger-warnings

Herman, J. L. (1992). Complex PTSD: A syndrome in survivors of prolonged and repeated trauma. *Journal of Traumatic Stress, 5*(3), 377–391.

———. (2015). *Trauma and recovery: The aftermath of violence—From domestic abuse to political terror.* Basic Books.

Herrington, A. (2002). Gone fishin': Rendering and the uses of personal experience in writing. In P. Belanoff, M. Dickson, C. I. Fontaine, & C. Moran (Eds.), *Writing with elbow,* (pp. 223–238). Utah State University Press.

Hobbes, T. (1962). *Leviathan: Or the matter, forme and power of a commonwealth, ecclesiasticall and civil*. Collier Books.

Hölzel, B. K., Carmody, J., Vangel, M., Congleton, C., Yerramsetti, S. M., Gard, T., & Lazar, S. W. (2011). Mindfulness practice leads to increases in regional brain gray matter density. *Psychiatry Research, 191*(1), 36–43. https://doi.org/10.1016/j.pscychresns.2010.08.006

Hosseini, K. (2003). *The kite runner.* Anchor Canada.

Howell, E. F. (2005). *The dissociative mind.* Routledge.

Howell, E. F., & Itzkowitz, S. (Eds.). (2016). *The dissociative mind in psychoanalysis: Understanding and working with trauma.* Routledge.

Inman, J. O., & Powell, R. A. (2018). In the absence of grades: Dissonance and desire in course-contract classrooms. *College Composition and Communication, 70*(1), 30–56.

Johnson, R. (2002, March). Friendly persuasion: Quaker pedagogy in a composition classroom [Paper presentation]. 53rd Conference on *College Composition and Communication*, Chicago, IL. https://files.eric.ed.gov/fulltext/ED463514.pdf

Jones, P. J., Bellet, B. W., & McNally, R. J. (2020). Helping or harming? The effect of trigger warnings on individuals with trauma histories. *Clinical Psychological Science, 8*(5), 905–917.

Kabat-Zinn, J. (2005). *Coming to our senses: Healing ourselves and the world through mindfulness.* Hachette Books.

———. (2013). *Full catastrophe living: Using the wisdom of your body and mind to face stress, pain, and illness*. Bantam.

Kamler, B. (2001). *Relocating the personal: A critical writing pedagogy.* SUNY Press.

Kasai, K., Yamasue, H., Gilbertson, M. W., Shenton, M. E., Rauch, S. L., & Pitman, R. K. (2008). Evidence for acquired pregenual anterior cingulate gray matter loss from a twin study of combat-related posttraumatic stress disorder. *Biological Psychiatry, 63*(6), 550–556. https://doi.org/10.1016/j.biopsych.2007.06.022

Kerr, C. E., Josyula, K., & Littenberg, R. (2011). Developing an observing attitude: An analysis of meditation diaries in an MBSR clinical trial. *Clinical Psychology & Psychotherapy, 18*(1), 80–93. https://doi.org/10.1002/cpp.700

Kerr, C. E., Sacchet, M. D., Lazar, S. W., Moore, C. I., & Jones, S. R. (2013). Mindfulness starts with the body: Somatosensory attention and top-down modulation of cortical alpha rhythms in mindfulness meditation. *Frontiers in Human Neuroscience, (7)*12, 1–15. https://doi.org/10.3389/fnhum.2013.00012

Kingsolver, B. (2013). *Animal dreams: A novel.* Harper Perennial.

Kinloch, V. (2009). *Harlem on our minds: Place, race, and the literacies of urban youth.* Teachers College Press.

Knox, E. (Ed.). (2017). *Trigger warnings: History, theory, context.* Rowman & Littlefield.

Kohut, H., & Goldberg, A. (1984). *How does analysis cure?* University of Chicago Press.

Kvale, S., & Brinkmann, S. (2009). *InterViews: Learning the craft of qualitative research interviewing.* Sage.

LaMay, B. C. (2016). *Personal narrative, revised: Writing love and agency in the high school classroom.* Teachers College Press.

Lanius, R. A., Terpou, B. A., & McKinnon, M. C. (2020). The sense of self in the aftermath of trauma: Lessons from the default mode network in posttraumatic stress disorder. European Journal of *Psychotraumatology, 11*(1), 1–12. https://doi.org/10.1080/20008198.2020.1807703

Lascelles, J. (2018). From the inside of an edge. In J. Hagemann, J. Lascelles, & K. Wedlock (Eds.), *Precipice: Writing at the edge* (pp. 133–138). Precipice Collective.

Lazar, S. W., Kerr, C. E., Wasserman, R. H., Gray, J. R., Greve, D. N., Treadway, M. T., McGarvey, M., Quinn, B. T., Dusek, J. A., Benson, H., Rauch, S. L., Moore, C. I., & Fischl, B. (2005). Meditation experience is associated with increased cortical thickness. *Neuroreport, 16*(17), 1893–1897. https://doi.org/10.1097/01.wnr.0000186598.66243.19

Lensmire, T. J. (2000). *Powerful writing, responsible teaching.* Teachers College Press.

Levine, P. A. (2010). *In an unspoken voice: How the body releases trauma and restores goodness.* North Atlantic Books.

Lewis, C. S. (1976). *Hamlet: The prince or the poem?* Norwood.

Luders, E., Kurth, F., Mayer, E. A., Toga, A. W., Narr, K. L., & Gaser, C. (2012). The unique brain anatomy of meditation practitioners: Alterations in cortical gyrification. *Frontiers in Human Neuroscience, (6)*34, 1–9. https://doi.org/10.3389/fnhum.2012.00034

Lukianoff, G., & Haidt, J. (2015, September). The coddling of the American mind. *The Atlantic.* http://www.theatlantic.com/magazine/archive/2015/09/the-coddling-ofthe-american-mind/399356

———. (2018). *The coddling of the American mind: How good intentions and bad ideas are setting up a generation for failure.* Penguin Press.

MacDevitt, J. (2013). Responding to student traumatic writing: A psychologist's view. *Teaching English in the Two Year College, 41*(2), 135–148.

Mack, P. (2014). *Healing deep hurt within: The transformational journey of a young patient undergoing regression therapy*. From the Heart Press.

Manne, K. (2015, September 19). Why I use trigger warnings. *The New York Times.* https://www.nytimes.com/2015/09/20/opinion/sunday/why-i-use-trigger-warnings.html

McLeod, K. (2002). *Wake up to your life: Discovering the Buddhist path of attention.* HarperOne.

McNally, R.J. (2016, September 13). If you need a trigger warning, you need P.T.S.D. Treatment. *TheNewYorkTimes.*https://www.nytimes.com/roomfordebate/2016/09/13/do-trigger-warnings-work/if-you-need-a-trigger-warning-you-need-ptsd-treatment

Medina, J. (2014, May 17). Warning: The literary canon could make students squirm. *The New York Times.* https://www.nytimes.com/2014/05/18/us/warning-the-literary-canon-could-make-students-squirm.html

Menakem, R. (2017). *My grandmother's hands: Racialized trauma and the pathway to mending our hearts and bodies.* Central Recovery Press.

Miller, A. (2019). *Death of a salesman.* Oxford University Press.

Murray, D. (1972). Teach writing as a process not product. *The Leaflet, 71*(3), 11–14.

Myers, K. A. (2016). Metanoic movement: The transformative power of regret. *College Composition and Communication, 67*(3), 385–410.

Nelson, J. D. (2016). Relational teaching with Black boys: Strategies for learning at a single-sex middle school for boys of color. *Teachers College Record, 118*(6), 1–30.

The New York Times. (2016, September 13). Do trigger warnings work? The New York Times. https://www.nytimes.com/roomfordebate/2016/09/13/do-trigger-warnings-work

Orr, T. (2017). *September 11 and terrorism in America.* Cherry Lake Publishing.

Owen, W. (2014). Dulce et decorum est. *The British Journal of Psychiatry, 204*(6), 461. https://doi.org/10.1192/bjp.bp.114.148304

Paley, K. S. (1996). The college application essay: A rhetorical paradox. *Assessing Writing, 3*(1), 85–105. https://doi.org/10.1016/S1075-2935(96)90005-7

Reichert, M., & Hawley, R. (2014). *I can learn from you: Boys as relational learners.* Harvard Education Press.

———. (2013). Relationships play primary role in boys' learning. *Phi Delta Kappan, 94*(8), 49–53. https://doi.org/10.1177/003172171309400812

Revanche, J. (2016, March 16). A history of trigger warnings, and the price and diversity of pain. *The Vocal.* https://medium.com/the-vocal/a-history-oftrigger-warnings-and-the-price-and-diversity-of-pain-ac8e796d0d70

Robinson, P. A. (Director). (1989). *Field of Dreams* [Film]. Universal Pictures.

Rodgers, C. R., & Raider-Roth, M. B. (2006). Presence in teaching. Teachers and Teaching: *Theory and Practice, 12*(3), 265–287. https://doi.org/10.1080/13450600500467548

Rogers, D. (2009). The working alliance in teaching and learning: Theoretical clarity and research implications. *International Journal for the Scholarship of Teaching & Learning, 3*(2), 1–9.

Roth, P. (2016). *American pastoral.* Vintage.

Rosenblatt, L. M. (1938). *Literature as exploration.* D. Appleton-Century.

Schaper, D. (2016, August 26). University of Chicago tells freshmen it does not support 'trigger warnings.' NPR. https://www.npr.org/2016/08/26/491531869/university-of-chicago-tells-freshmen-it-does-not-support-trigger-warnings

Shakespeare, W. (2019). *Hamlet: Prince of Denmark* (P. Edwards & H. Hirschfeld, Eds.). Cambridge University Press.

———. (2020). *Shakespeare's sonnets* (B. A. Mowat & P. Werstine, Eds.). Simon & Schuster.

———. (2004). *The tragedy of Macbeth* (B. A. Mowat, P. Werstine, & S. Snyder, Eds.). Washington Square Press.

Shapiro, S. L., Astin, J. A., Bishop, S. R., & Cordova, M. (2005). Mindfulness-based stress reduction for health care professionals: Results from a randomized trial. *International Journal of Stress Management, 12*(2), 164–176. https://doi.org/10.1037/1072-5245.12.2.164

Shapiro, S. L., Oman, D., Thoresen, C. E., Plante, T. G., & Flinders, T. (2008). Cultivating mindfulness: Effects on well-being. *Journal of Clinical Psychology, 64*(7), 840–862.

Sharp, P. B., Sutton, B. P., Paul, E. J., Sherepa, N., Hillman, C. H., Cohen, N. J., Kramer, A. F., Prakash, R. S., Heller, W., Telzer, E. H., & Barbey, A. K. (2018). Mindfulness training induces structural connectome changes in insula networks. *Scientific Reports, 8*(1), 1–10. https://doi.org/10.1038/s41598-018-26268-w

Sheline, Y. I. (2000). 3D MRI studies of neuroanatomic changes in unipolar major depression: The role of stress and medical comorbidity. *Biological Psychiatry, 48*(8), 791–800. https://doi.org/10.1016/S0006-3223(00)00994-X

Singleton, O., Hölzel, B. K., Vangel, M., Brach, N., Carmody, J., & Lazar, S. W. (2014). Change in brainstem gray matter concentration following a mindfulness-based intervention is correlated with improvement in psychological well-being. *Frontiers in Human Neuroscience, (8)*33, 1–7. https://doi.org/10.3389/fnhum.2014.00033

Smagorinsky, P. (2019). *Teaching English by design: How to create and carry out instructional units.* Heinemann.

Stolorow, R. D. (2007). *Trauma and human existence: Implications for Heidegger's conception of Mitsein* [Doctoral dissertation], University of California. ProQuest.

Suzuki, S. (2006). *Zen mind, beginner's mind.* Shambhala Library.

Tamas, S. (2009). Writing and righting trauma: Troubling the autoethnographic voice. *Forum: Qualitative Social Research, 10*(1). https://doi.org/10.17169/fqs-10.1.1211

Taren, A. A., Gianaros, P. J., Greco, C. M., Lindsay, E. K., Fairgrieve, A., Brown, K. W., Rosen, R. K., Ferris, J. L., Julson, E., Marsland, A. L., Bursley, J. K., Ramsburg, J., & Creswell, J. D. (2015). Mindfulness meditation training alters stress-related amygdala resting state functional connectivity: A randomized controlled trial. *Social Cognitive and Affective Neuroscience, 10*(12), 1758–1768. https://doi.org/10.1093/scan/nsv066

Teasdale, J. D. (1999). Metacognition, mindfulness and the modification of mood disorders. *Clinical Psychology and Psychotherapy, 6*(2), 146–155.

Tippett, K. (Host). (2020, April 30). A life worthy of our breath [Audio podcast episode]. In *On Being*. American Public Media. https://onbeing.org/programs/ocean-vuong-a-life-worthy-of-our-breath/

Treleaven, D. (2018). *Trauma-sensitive mindfulness: Practices for safe and transformative healing.* W. W. Norton & Company.

———. (Producer.) (2020). *The truth about mindfulness and trauma: How to mitigate risks and promote healing for trauma survivors.* [Video]. https://davidtreleaven.com/webinar/

Turley, E. D., & Gallagher, C. W. (2008). On the "uses" of rubrics: Reframing the great rubric debate. *English Journal, 97*(4), 87–92.

Umbach, M., & Hüppauf, B. (2005). *Vernacular modernism: Heimat, globalization, and the built environment.* Stanford University Press.

van der Kolk, B. A. (2015). *The body keeps the score: Brain, mind, and body in the healing of trauma.* Penguin Books.

Van Overwalle, F. (2009). Social cognition and the brain: A meta-analysis. *Human Brain Mapping, 30*(3), 829–858. https://doi.org/10.1002/hbm.20547

Vidali, A. (2007). Performing the rhetorical freak show: Disability, student writing, and college admissions. *College English, 69*(6), 615–641.

Warren, J. (2013). The rhetoric of college application essays: Removing obstacles for low income and minority students. *American Secondary Education, 42*(1), 43–56.

Weng, H. Y., Ikeda, M. P., Lewis-Peacock, J. A., Chao, M. T., Fullwiley, D., Goldman, V., Skinner, S., Duncan, L. G., Gazzaley, A., & Hecht, F. M. (2020). Toward a compassionate intersectional neuroscience: Increasing diversity and equity in contemplative neuroscience. *Frontiers in Psychology, 11*(573134), 1–16. https://doi.org/10.3389/fpsyg.2020.573134

Wentzel, K. R. (1997). Student motivation in middle school: The role of perceived pedagogical caring. *Journal of Educational Psychology, 89*(3), 411–419. https://doi.org/10.1037/0022-0663.89.3.411

Wilhelm, J. D. (1997) *"You gotta BE the book": Teaching engaged and reflective reading with adolescents.* Teachers College Press.

Williams, T. (2004). *A streetcar named Desire; With an introduction by Arthur Miller*. New Directions.

Winn, M. T. (2013). Toward a restorative English education. *Research in the Teaching of English, 48*(1), 126–135.

Wissman, K., & Vasudevan, L. (2012). Re-writing the stock stories of urban adolescents. In D. E. Alvermann & K. A. Hinchman (Eds.), *Reconceptualizing the literacies in adolescents' lives: Bridging the everyday/academic divide* (pp. 160–180). Routledge.

Wissman, K. K., & Wiseman, A. M. (2011). "That's my worst nightmare": Poetry and trauma in the middle school classroom. *Pedagogies: An International Journal, 6*(3), 234–249. https://doi.org/10.1080/1554480X.2011.579051

Wolfsdorf, A. (2021). *Conceit upon her father. In Humanizing Grief in Higher Education* (pp. 31–37). https://doi.org/10.4324/9780429326493-4

———. (2021). Gazing at the skull: Teaching Hamlet during the pandemic of 2020. *English Journal, 110*(6), 93–95.

———. (2017). Reflecting on functioning in trigger happy America. *Changing English, 24*(3), pp. 299–317. https://doi.org/10.1080/1358684x.2017.1331119

———. (2018). When it comes to high school English, let's put away the triggers. The *English Journal, 108*(1), 39–44.

Wolfsdorf, A., Scott, A., & Herzog, S. (2019). What happened on July 21st: An investigation of trauma and trigger warnings in the English classroom. *Changing English, 26*(2), 198–215. https://doi.org/10.1080/1358684x.2018.1552514

Varela, F., Thompson, E., & Rosch, E. (1991). *The embodied mind: Cognitive science and human experience.* The MIT Press.

Yagelski, R. P. (2009). A thousand writers writing: Seeking change through the radical practice of writing as a way of being. *English Education, 42*(1), 6–28.

Zegers, K. (2019, April 19). By the numbers: School shootings since Columbine. *NECN.* https://www.necn.com/news/national-international/school-shootings-since-columbine/1908046/

Zeidan, F., Grant, J. A., Brown, C. A., McHaffie, J. G., & Coghill, R. C. (2012). Mindfulness meditation-related pain relief: Evidence for unique brain mechanisms in the regulation of pain. *Neuroscience Letters, 520*(2), 165–173. https://doi.org/10.1016/j.neulet.2012.03.082

Zembylas, M. (2006). Witnessing in the classroom: The ethics and politics of affect. *Educational Theory, 56*(3), 305–324. https://doi.org/10.1111/j.1741-5446.2006.00228.x

Index

Note: An 'f' following a page number indicates a figure.

About the Authors

Adam Wolfsdorf is the Humanities Department chair and an original founding member of Bay Ridge Preparatory High School. He is also an adjunct professor at New York University's Steinhardt School of Education, and a visiting assistant professor in Wesleyan University's Graduate Liberal Studies Program. Wolfsdorf holds a PhD in English education from Columbia University, where he served as the coordinator of the INSTEP master's program. He has published extensively in *Changing English, The F. Scott Fitzgerald Review, English Education, English Journal,* and *The Columbia Literary Journal.* Wolfsdorf has book chapters in *Humanizing Grief in Higher Education* (Routledge) and *Deep Reading,* Volume 2 (Peter Lang). Outside of the English classroom, Wolfsdorf has performed professionally for 25 years. He appeared in the national tours of the Broadway musicals *RENT* (with Neil Patrick Harris) and *Grease.* He also fronts the nationally touring rock band, The Energy (MTV, NBC, ABC, and ESPN). Wolfsdorf earned his master's degree in psychology and education from Columbia University, and holds a bachelor's degree in English from Harvard University.

Kristen Park Wedlock researches, teaches, and practices contemplative writing in the dharma arts tradition of Chogyam Trungpa Rinpoche, Allen Ginsberg, Anne Waldman, Reed Bye, and Bhanu Kapil. Her background in physiology, kinesiology, dance, and somatic yoga informs the way she composes the page: a choreography of words excavated from the body. She serves as an assistant professor of writing at Georgian Court University. Additionally, she is cofounder of Precipice Collective, a small press designed to serve its community through alternative models of investigative, sustainable, critical research; collaborative, integrative publishing; and engaged, embodied outreach. Her book-length publications include *Strangers at the Event Horizon* (Gesture Press), and *Precipice: Writing at the Edge* (Precipice Collective). Kristen claimed her master's degree in fine arts in writing and poetics from Naropa University, as well as her Bachelor of Science in exercise science from Rutgers University. In addition to her formal education, she earned a certificate from the Contemplative Studies ICP Summer Program at Brown University, a 200-hour Teacher Certificate in Soma Yoga and Movement Re-Education from the Princeton Center for Yoga and Health, and an Integrative Somatic Therapy Certificate from the Embody Lab.

Cassandra Lo, EdD is an assistant professor of English education and literacy at St. Thomas Aquinas College in Sparkill, New York. She earned a doctorate in education in reading, writing, and literacy from the University of Pennsylvania, a Master of Arts degree in English education from Teachers College, Columbia University, and a Bachelor of Arts degree in English and teacher education from the College of the Holy Cross. A former high school English and journalism teacher, Dr. Lo now works with both literacy specialists and preservice teachers in methodology coursework and the student teaching seminar. Her research focuses on relational teaching practices, trauma-sensitive pedagogies, and supporting teachers of color. Dr. Lo has been published in *School Psychology Quarterly* and *Writing and Pedagogy* and has a chapter in *Developing Trauma Informed Teachers* (InfoAge). She has presented her work at conferences for many educational organizations, including NCTE, AERA, LRA, and NASPA.

This book was typeset in TheMix and Palatino by Cynthia Gomez.

The typeface used on the cover is Cinzel.

The book was printed on 50-lb. white offset paper by Ingram.